TRUTH SPOKEN IN LOVE

J. C. Ryle at his desk in later years

Ryle entered the ministry of the Church of England in 1841. He served for many years as a parish minister, and then as the first Bishop of Liverpool from 1880 to 1900.

TRUTH SPOKEN IN LOVE

An Anthology of Quotations from

J. C. RYLE

Compiled by

Daniel W. McManigal

THE BANNER OF TRUTH TRUST

THE BANNER OF TRUTH TRUST

Head Office
3 Murrayfield Road
Edinburgh, EH12 6EL
UK

North America Office
610 Alexander Spring Road
Carlisle, PA 17015
USA

banneroftruth.org

*

ISBN
Print: 978 1 80040 554 7
Epub: 978 1 80040 555 4

*

Typeset in 11/15 pt Adobe Garamond Pro
at The Banner of Truth Trust, Edinburgh

Printed in the USA by
Versa Press, Inc.,
East Peoria, IL

CONTENTS

INTRODUCTION

'Of the making of many books, there is no end' (Eccles. 12:12). What you are holding in your hand is not so much an illustration of the inspired statement—though it is that—but, rather, a topical guide to the many volumes of timeless wisdom and practical insights of one of the great champions of biblical truth.

I first became aware of the writings of J. C. Ryle (1816–1900) in my father's study. Among the books lining his shelves was Ryle's *Holiness: Its Nature, Hindrances, Difficulties and Roots*. I did not begin reading it at that time, sadly, but I do recall looking at the chapter headings and thinking that I should. This thought would bear fruit years later in the midst of a busy preaching and teaching ministry.

Pastors and teachers should consult the written wisdom of the past for deeper understanding of the biblical truths they are preparing to explain in the present. In the writings of J. C. Ryle readers have found faithful biblical wisdom and searching applications that aim at the heart. Such were the gifts the Spirit gave him. 'The characteristics of Bishop Ryle's method and style are obvious,' wrote Dr Martyn Lloyd-Jones. 'He is pre-eminently and always scriptural and expository. He never starts with a theory into which he tries to fit various scriptures. He always starts with the word and expounds it. It is exposition at its very best and highest. It is always clear and logical and invariably leads to a clear enunciation of doctrine.'[1] Ryle's

[1] D. Martyn Lloyd-Jones, 'Foreword,' in *Holiness: Its Nature, Hindrances, Difficulties and Roots* (Cambridge: James Clarke & Co Ltd, 1977), iii.

expositions of Scripture and articulation of biblical doctrines were equally well-informed by the writings of the great theologians of the past. One need only glance through the notes of his *Expository Thoughts on the Gospels* to see that he took time to study the reasoned positions of others, before putting his own to paper.

Not only were biblical fidelity and practical applications hallmarks of his work, but the doctrines he unfolded often came in lively, vivid, and memorable language. His writing has been described as having a 'brisk, blunt style, pungent and persuasive, made up of short, abrupt, in-your-face sentences.'[1] Ryle wasted no words and used no filler materials to pad his arguments and exhortations. What he pressed upon aspiring preachers, he himself practised in the pulpit and also in the study. 'He is the best speaker who can turn the ear into an eye.'[2] His books, many of which are compilations of tracts reworked from sermons, are illustrative of this conviction. He honed his God-given skills in such a way so as to make deep truths accessible to broad audiences and with a sense of urgency.[3] As J. I. Packer observed, 'his down-to-earth illustrations and rhetorical emphases gave a sense of the drama, the dangers, the challenges, glories and joys of life under the eye and hand of the God of the gospel; and thus, in a word, he communicated brilliantly at [the] popular level.'[4] The net result is that more than one hundred years after the first Bishop of Liverpool's entrance into glory on 10 June 1900, those who read him will be anything but disappointed. It is the aim of this anthology to encourage readers, old and new alike, to pick up Ryle's many volumes and spiritually profit from them.

[1] J. I. Packer, *Faithfulness and Holiness: The Witness of J. C. Ryle* (Wheaton: Crossway, 2002), 61.

[2] J. C. Ryle, *Simplicity in Preaching* (Edinburgh: The Banner of Truth Trust, 2010), 16-17.

[3] According to Iain Murray, Ryle did not find preaching easy and confessed that he had not learned to preach until after the age of fifty. Iain H. Murray, *J. C. Ryle, Prepared to Stand Alone* (Edinburgh: The Banner of Truth Trust, 2016), 59.

[4] Packer, *Faithfulness and Holiness,* 61.

Reflecting back on the many hours reading thousands of his pages, if there were two things that stand out like jewels in his crown, they were Ryle's unflagging determination to tell us the terrible truth about ourselves, and to point us to Jesus. And this, after all, is what faithful ministers of the gospel aim to do (Acts 5:42; Rom. 15:20; 1 Cor. 1:23; Phil. 1:18), yes, *must* do. In this, the great expounder of biblical truth is a faithful example for us to follow.

To pastors and teachers of God's word, it is my hope that this selection of quotations will prove useful in your studies and helpful in your teaching and preaching. If new generations of pastors, Bible students, teachers, and, indeed, believers in general are introduced to Ryle's writings through this book, I will be grateful to have played a small part in pointing the way.

There have been a number of people who have encouraged me in the creation of this anthology. Were it not for the help of David Davis giving me many of the Banner of Truth's volumes of Ryle, and the encouragement of Jeremy Baker, Weston Stoler, Clayton Willis, Bulut Yasar and others with whom I shared so many Ryle quotations, this work may have remained on my laptop's hard drive for my own personal benefit and that of the congregations I served. I am particularly grateful to my family for giving me the extra time to read and compile this book of quotes, and to Rev. Jonathan Watson, the Banner of Truth's senior editor, for his kind encouragement.

Daniel W. McManigal
Florida
May 2025

Note

Titles of books and page references provided after each quotation refer to the Banner of Truth editions detailed in the bibliography on page 219.

ADAM

To the blood of Adam we owe the beginning of our deadly spiritual ailment. To the blood of Christ alone must we all look for a cure.

Upper Room, 79.

ADOPTION

Those whom God adopts he teaches and trains.

Practical Religion, 387.

AFFECTIONS

Feelings, no doubt, fill a most important office in our personal Christianity. Without them there can be no saving religion. Hope, and joy, and peace, and confidence, and resignation, and love, and fear, are things which must be felt, if they really exist. But it must never be forgotten that there are religious affections, which are spurious and false, and spring from nothing better than animal excitement. It is quite possible to feel great pleasure, or deep alarm, under the preaching of the gospel, and yet to be utterly destitute of the grace of God. The tears of some hearers of sermons, and the extravagant delight of others, are no certain marks of conversion.

Expository Thoughts on Luke, 1.192.

Just as the new spring buds in a beech hedge push off the old leaves and make them quietly fall to the ground, so does the new heart of a believer invariably affect his tastes and likings, and make him drop many things which he once loved and lived in, because he now likes them no more.

Practical Religion, 286.

Truly it is poor work to set our affections on a dying world and its short lived comforts, and for the sake of an inch of time to lose a glorious immortality!

Practical Religion, 304.

AFFLICTIONS

Affliction is one of God's medicines. By it he often teaches lessons which would be learned in no other way.

Expository Thoughts on John, 1.178.

Every sickness and sorrow is the voice of God speaking to us. Each has its peculiar message.

Expository Thoughts on John, 1.188.

The veil is drawn over their joy, though it was not over their sorrow. Affliction is a more profitable study than rejoicing.

Expository Thoughts on John, 2.211
(also *Power and Sympathy of Christ,* 101).

Let us firmly believe at the worst of times, that every step in our lives is ordered by the Lord, with perfect wisdom and perfect love, and that we shall see it all at last. Let us not doubt that he is always doing all things well. He is good in giving, and equally good in taking away.

Upper Room, 229.

ANGELS

They know what misery sin has brought into creation. They know the blessedness of heaven, and the privilege of an open door into it.—Above all, it shows us the deep love and compassion which the angels feel towards poor lost man. They rejoice in the glorious prospect of many souls being saved, and many brands plucked from the burning.

Let us strive to be more like-minded with the angels.

Expository Thoughts on Luke, 1.44-45.

APOSTLES

Let it be carefully noted, that, speaking literally and accurately, there is no such thing as apostolical succession. The office of the apostles was isolated, peculiar, and distinct, and ceased with themselves. Ministers of the churches of Christ are successors of Timothy and Titus, but not of the apostles.

Expository Thoughts on Luke, 1.224-25.

Three times we have sins against charity recorded in the Gospels as committed by John. Once we find him and his brother asking to sit at Christ's right and left hand in his kingdom, and to be preferred before all the other apostles. Once we find him forbidding a man to cast out devils, because he did not follow the apostles. Here again we find him showing a fierce and cruel spirit against the Samaritan villagers for not receiving our Lord. Yet this was the apostle who proved at last most remarkable for preaching love and charity. No change is too great for the Lord to work.

Expository Thoughts on Luke, 1.256.

APOSTASY

All are not Israel which are called Israel. Men may have feelings, desires, convictions, resolutions, hopes, joys, sorrows in religion, and yet never have the grace of God. They may run well for a season, and bid fair to reach heaven, and yet break down entirely after a time, go back to the world, and end like Demas, Judas Iscariot, and Lot's wife.

Expository Thoughts on John, 1.292.

The heart is always deceitful and desperately wicked; the devil is always busy, and seeking whom he may devour; the world is always ensnaring; the way of life is narrow, the enemies many, the friends few, the difficulties great, the cross heavy, the doctrine of the gospel offensive to the natural man. What thoughtful person need wonder that multitudes in every age go back from Christ?

Upper Room, 167.

ASSURANCE

All God's children have faith; not all have assurance. I think this ought never to be forgotten.

Holiness, 144.

He must know what it is simply to *believe* and to be justified by faith before he can expect to feel assured.

Holiness, 159.

Our sense of salvation depends much on the manner of our living.

Holiness, 162.

Paul never saw the Book of Life, and yet Paul says, 'I know and am persuaded.'

Holiness, 166.

The least spark of grace shall prove as unquenchable as the most burning and shining light. Your faith may be very feeble, your grace may be very weak, your strength may be very small, you may feel that in spiritual things you are but a child. You may doubt the reality of your own conversion. Yet fear not, neither be afraid. It is not on the quantity of a man's grace, but on the truth and genuineness of it that the promise turns.

Old Paths, 451.

False Assurance

We may be washed in the waters of baptism, and yet know nothing of the water of life. We may go to the Lord's table every Sunday of our lives, and yet never eat Christ's body and drink Christ's blood by faith. Miserable indeed is our condition if we can say nothing more than this! We possess nothing but the outside of Christianity: we are leaning on a reed.

Old Paths, 95.

Uncertainty of Salvation

The fires of hell are before you, and you are uncertain whether your soul is insured. This world below must soon be left, and you are uncertain whether you have a mansion prepared to receive you in the world above. The judgment will soon be set, and you are uncertain whether you have an Advocate to plead your cause. Eternity will soon begin, and you are uncertain whether you are prepared to meet God. Oh, sit down this day, and study the subject of salvation! Give God no rest till uncertainty has disappeared, and you have got hold of a reasonable hope that you are saved.

Old Paths, 84.

ATHEIST

Little does the infidel think, as he lies sick in some of our great hospitals, that he owes all his present comforts to the very book he affects to despise. Had it not been for the Bible, he might have died in misery, uncared for, unnoticed, and alone.

Light from Old Times, 9.

ATONEMENT

Christ … did not come on earth to be a conqueror, or a philosopher, or a mere teacher of morality. He came to save sinners. He came to do that which man could never do for himself,—to do that which money and learning can never obtain,—to do that which is essential to man's real happiness: he came to 'take away sin.

Expository Thoughts on John, 1.40.

The payment that he made on the cross was more than enough to make satisfaction for the debts of all. The blood that he shed was precious enough to wash away the sins of all. His atonement on the cross was sufficient for all mankind, though efficient only to those who believe. The sin that he took up and bore on the cross was the sin of the whole world.

Expository Thoughts on John, 1.40-41.

We are all in a wilderness. We must feed on Christ crucified, and the atonement made by his death, or we shall die in our sins.

Expository Thoughts on John, 1.230.

When our Lord says, 'I will give my flesh,' it appears to me that he can only mean 'I will give it to die, to suffer, to be offered up on the cross as a sacrifice for sin.' When our Lord says, 'I will give my flesh *for the life* of the world,' I believe he means, 'I will give my body to death on account of, for the sake of, to procure, purchase, and obtain the life of the world. I will give my death to procure the world's life. My death shall be the ransom, the payment, and the redemption-money by which eternal life shall be purchased for a world of sinners.'

Expository Thoughts on John, 1.275.

For whom, do you suppose, was all that suffering undergone, which Jesus endured at Calvary? Why was the holy Son of God dealt with as a malefactor, reckoned a transgressor, and condemned to so cruel a death? For whom were those hands and feet nailed to the cross? For whom was that side pierced with the spear? For whom did that precious blood flow so freely down? Wherefore was all this done? It was done for you!

Old Paths, 53.

For our sins, as our Substitute, he gave himself, suffered, and died,—the just for the unjust, the innocent for the guilty,—that he might deliver us from the curse of a broken law, and provide a complete pardon for all who are willing to receive it.

Old Paths, 175-76.

For what end and purpose did the Father give his only begotten Son? Was it only to supply an example of self-denial and self-sacrifice? No! It was for a far higher end and purpose than this. He gave him to be a sacrifice for man's sin, and an atonement for man's transgression. He gave him to be delivered for our offences, and to die for the ungodly. He gave him to bear our iniquities, and to suffer for our sins, the just for the unjust. He gave him to be made a curse for us, that we might be redeemed from the curse of the law. He gave him to be sin for us who knew no sin, that we might be made the righteousness of God in him.

Old Paths, 360.

Hold fast the faith once delivered to the saints,—that the special object for which Christ was given was to die for sinners, and to make atonement for them by his sacrifice on the cross. Once give up this great doctrine, and there is little worth contending for in Christianity. If Christ did not really 'bear our sins on the tree' as our Substitute, there is an end of all solid peace (1 Pet. 2:24).

Old Paths, 360-61.

He shed his blood on the cross for all, but he only washes those who have part in him. He invites all, but he quickens whom he will, and brings them to glory.

Upper Room, 234.

Atonement and Intercession

The first work he did on earth when he died upon the cross: the second work he carries on in heaven, at the right hand of God the Father.—The first work he did for all mankind, and offers the benefit of it to all the world: the second work he carries on and accomplishes solely and entirely on behalf of his own elect, his people, his believing servants, and his children.

Old Paths, 413.

Limited Atonement

I confess, boldly, that I hold the doctrine of particular redemption, in a certain sense, as strongly as anyone. I believe that none are *effectually* redeemed but God's elect. They, and they only, are set free from the guilt, and power, and consequences of sin. But I hold no less strongly, that Christ's work of atonement is *sufficient* for all mankind. There is a sense in which he has tasted death for every man, and has taken upon him the sin of the world (Heb. 2:9; John 1:29).

Old Paths, 361.

BACKSLIDING

I do believe that a man may fall away so far that he shall lose sight of his own grace, and despair of his own salvation. And if this is not hell, it is certainly the next thing to it! A wounded conscience, a mind sick of itself, a memory full of self-reproach, a heart pierced through with the Lord's arrows, a spirit broken with a load of inward accusation,—all this is *a taste of hell.*

Practical Religion, 73.

When a backslider was pointed out to him [Daniel Rowland], who had once been one of his followers, he said: 'It is to be feared indeed that he is one of *my* disciples; for had he been one of *my Lord's* disciples, he would not have been in such a state of sin and rebellion.'

Christian Leaders of the Eighteenth Century, 195.

The story of Peter's fall teaches us, firstly, *how small and gradual are the steps by which men may go down into great sins.*

The various steps in Peter's fall are clearly marked out by the Gospel writers. ... The first step was proud self-confidence. Though all men denied Christ, yet he never would! He was ready to go with Him both to prison and to death!—The second step was indolent neglect of prayer. When his Master told him to pray, lest he should enter into temptation, he gave way to drowsiness, and was found asleep.—The third step was vacillating indecision. When the enemies of Christ came upon him, Peter first fought, then ran away, then turned again, and finally 'followed afar off.'—The fourth step was mingling with bad company. He went into the high priest's house and sat among the servants by the fire, trying to conceal his religion, and hearing and seeing all manner of evil.—The fifth and last step was the natural consequence of the preceding four. He was overwhelmed with fear when suddenly charged with being a disciple. The snare was round his neck. He could not escape. He plunged deeper into error than ever. He denied his blessed Master three times. The mischief, be it remembered, had been done before. The denial was only the disease coming to a head.

Expository Thoughts on Luke, 2.324-25.

BAPTISM

It cannot be neglected or despised without great sin. When rightly used, with faith and prayer, it is calculated to convey the highest blessings.

Expository Thoughts on John, 1.134.

Baptism and the Lord's supper will always be most truly reverenced in those churches where the truth as it is in Jesus is most fully taught and known.

Expository Thoughts on John, 1.134-35.

I should find it very hard to believe that the three thousand baptized on the day of Pentecost, or the jailor and his family, baptized at midnight in the Philippian prison, were all immersed.

Expository Thoughts on John, 1.125.

Baptism cannot be a thing of slight importance, if Christ himself was baptized. The use of baptism would never have been enjoined on the church of Christ, if it had been a mere outward form, incapable of conveying any blessing.

Expository Thoughts on Luke, 1.78.

Baptism is an ordinance of great simplicity. The outward part or sign is water, administered in the name of the Father, the Son, and the Holy Ghost, or in the name of Christ. The inward part, or thing signified, is that washing in the blood of Christ, and inward cleansing of the heart by the Holy Ghost, without which no one can be saved.

Knots Untied, 98.

It is unreasonable to suppose that the Lord Jesus, the great Head of the church, would solemnly appoint an ordinance which was to be as useless to the soul as a mere human enrolment or an act of civil registration.

Knots Untied, 98-99.

Is not the world, then, one of the three great foes which you were solemnly bound at baptism to resist?

Upper Room, 121.

It is quite certain that St Paul wrote his Epistles in the New Testament to the churches upon this principle. He constantly addresses their members as 'saints' and 'elect,' and as having grace, and faith, and hope, and love, though it is evident that some of them had no grace at all! I am firmly convinced that the compilers of our Prayer Book drew up its services upon the same lines, the lines of charitable supposition; and it is on this principle alone that the book can be interpreted, and especially on the subject of Baptism and Regeneration.

Upper Room, 315.

Baptism with Fire

['Baptize with fire'.] The meaning of this expression is doubtful, and has never been fully cleared up. Some confine it entirely to the descent of the Holy Ghost on the day of Pentecost, when 'cloven tongues like as of fire' sat upon each person present on the occasion (Acts 2:3.). Others confine it entirely to the converting operation of the Holy Ghost, purifying and refining the heart as fire purifieth gold. Both views are probably included.

Expository Thoughts on Luke, 1.76.

Baptismal Regeneration

We are expressly told that Simon the sorcerer, after his baptism, had 'no part' in Christ, and his 'heart was not right in the sight of God.' Simon, therefore, could not have been regenerated, or born again in baptism (Acts 8:21).

Upper Room, 307-8.

No religious statement is *kind* and charitable which is not strictly true. To keep back any part of God's truth, in order to appear kind, is not only a mistake but a sin. The way to do good is to warn people plainly, that they must not suppose they are regenerate because they are baptized.

Upper Room, 312.

Myriads are every year brought to the font, and solemnly baptized in the name of the Trinity, who serve sin like slaves, and neglect Christ all their days. Wretched indeed is that man's state of soul who can give no better evidence of his citizenship of heaven than the mere naked fact of his baptism!

Practical Religion, 209.

Infant Baptism

There is no greater mistake than to suppose that infants, by reason of their tender age, are incapable of being operated upon by the Holy Spirit. The manner of his work upon a little child's heart, is undoubtedly mysterious and incomprehensible. But so also are all his works upon the sons of men. Let us beware of limiting God's power and compassion. He is a merciful God. With him nothing is impossible.

Let us remember these things in connection with the subject of infant baptism. It is a feeble objection to say that infants ought not to be baptized, because they cannot repent and believe. If an infant can be filled with the Holy Ghost, he is surely not unworthy to be admitted into the visible church.

Expository Thoughts on Luke, 1.11.

Some think that children ought to be baptized, as a matter of course, and that if they die unbaptized they cannot be saved. Others think that children ought not to be baptized, but can give no satisfactory reason why they think so.—Some think that all children are regenerate by virtue of their baptism. Others seem to think that children are incapable of receiving any grace, and that they ought not to be enrolled in the church till they are grown up.—Some think that children are naturally innocent, and would do no wickedness unless they learned it from others. Others think that it is no use to expect them to be converted when young, and that they must be treated as unbelievers till they come to years of discretion.—All these opinions appear to be errors, in one direction or another. All are to be deprecated, for all lead to many painful mistakes.

Expository Thoughts on Luke, 2.197-98.

If Jewish children were not too young to be circumcised in the Old Testament dispensation, it is exceedingly hard to understand why Christian children should be too young to be baptized under the gospel. Thousands of children, no doubt, receive no benefit from baptism.

Expository Thoughts on Luke, 2.198.

To suppose that Christ will admit them into his glorified church, and yet maintain that he would not have them in his professing church on earth, is an inconsistency which can never be explained.

Expository Thoughts on Luke, 2.198-99.

Children were *admitted into the Old Testament Church by a formal ordinance*, from the time of Abraham downwards. That ordinance was circumcision. It was an ordinance which God himself appointed, and the neglect of which was denounced as a great sin. It was an ordinance about which the highest language is used in the New Testament. St Paul calls it 'a seal of the righteousness of faith' (Rom. 4:11). Now, if children were considered to be capable of admission into the church by an ordinance in the Old Testament, it is difficult to see why they cannot be admitted in the New. The general tendency of the gospel is to increase men's spiritual privileges and not to diminish them. Nothing, I believe, would astonish a Jewish convert so much as to tell him his children could *not* be baptized! 'If they are fit to receive circumcision,' he would reply, 'why are they not fit to receive baptism?'

Knots Untied, 109.

That infants were formally admitted into the church by an outward ordinance, for 1,800 years before Christ came, is a fact that cannot be denied. Now, if he had meant to change the practice, and exclude infants from baptism, I should expect to find some plain text about it. But I find none, and therefore I conclude that there was to be no alteration and no change. The very *absence* of any direct command, on which the Baptists lay such stress, is, in reality, one of the strongest arguments against them! No change and therefore no text!

Knots Untied, 112-13.

The absence of some plain text or command is not a sufficient argument against infant baptism. There are not a few things which can be proved and inferred from Scripture, though they are not plainly and directly taught. Let the Baptist show us a single plain text which directly warrants the admission of women to the Lord's Supper.

Knots Untied, 113.

He that would do honour to baptism should maintain that it is a high and holy ordinance, which, like every ordinance appointed by Christ, ought not to be touched without solemn reverence; and that no blessing can be expected unless it is used with heart, and knowledge, and faith, and prayer, and followed by godly training of the child baptized.

Upper Room, 310.

Mode of Baptism

I can find nothing in the Bible to warrant the assertion that either dipping, or pouring, or sprinkling, is *essential* to baptism. I believe it would be impossible to prove that either way of baptizing is exclusively right, or that either is downright wrong. So long as water is used in the name of the Trinity, the precise mode of administering the ordinance is left an open question.

Knots Untied, 102.

The three thousand baptized in one day at the feast of Pentecost (Acts 2:41),—the jailor at Philippi suddenly baptized at midnight in prison (Acts 16:33)—is it at all likely or probable that they were all 'dipped'?

Knots Untied, 103.

BAXTER, RICHARD

He always spoke like one who saw God, and felt death at his back.

Light from Old Times, 283.

When a friend comforted him with the remembrance of the good many had received from his writings, he replied, 'I was but pen in God's hand, and what praise is due to a pen?'

Light from Old Times, 293.

BIBLE

Ignorance of the Scriptures is the root of all error.

Expository Thoughts on John, 1.214.

If the Bible is anything at all it is the statute-book of God's kingdom, the code of laws and regulations by which the subjects of that kingdom are to live, the register-deed of the terms on which they have peace now and shall have glory hereafter.

Is All Scripture Inspired? 29.

If you have not yet found out that Christ crucified is the foundation of the whole volume, you have read your Bible hitherto to very little profit. Your religion is a heaven without a sun, an arch without a key-stone, a compass without a needle, a clock without spring or weights, a lamp without oil.

Old Paths, 233.

There is hardly a step in man's life, from childhood to old age, hardly any position in which man can be placed, for which the Bible has not held out encouragement to everyone who desires to do right in the sight of God. There are 'shalls' and 'wills' in God's treasury for every condition. About God's infinite mercy and compassion—about his readiness to receive all who repent and believe—about his willingness to forgive, pardon, and absolve the chief of sinners—about his power to change hearts and alter our corrupt nature—about the encouragements to pray, and hear the gospel, and draw near to the throne of grace—about strength for duty, comfort in trouble, guidance in perplexity, help in sickness, consolation in death, support under bereavement, happiness beyond the grave, reward in glory—about all these things there is an abundant supply of promises in the Word.

Holiness, 363.

Let us strive, every year we live, to become more deeply acquainted with Scripture. Let us study it, search into it, dig into it, meditate on it, until it dwell in us richly (Col. 3:16). In particular, let us labour to make ourselves familiar with those parts of the Bible which, like the book of Psalms, describe the experience of the saints of old. We shall find it most helpful to us in all our approaches to God. It will supply us with the best and most suitable language both for the expression of our wants and thanksgivings.

Expository Thoughts on Luke, 1.27.

There is a fullness about the whole Book, which is a strong proof of its inspiration. The more we read it, the more it will seem to contain. All other books become threadbare, if they are constantly read. Their weak points, and their shallowness become every year more apparent. The Bible alone seems broader, and deeper, and fuller, the oftener it is studied.

Expository Thoughts on Luke, 2.257.

The Bible alone gives a *true and faithful account of man.* It does not flatter him as novels and romances do; it does not conceal his faults and exaggerate his goodness; it paints him just as he is.

Is All Scripture Inspired? 7.

It exactly meets the heart of man in every rank or class, in every country and climate, in every age and period of life. It is the only book in existence which is never out of place and out of date.

Is All Scripture Inspired? 16.

What greater insult to God can a man be guilty of than to refuse to read the letter God sends him from heaven?

Old Paths, 28.

God has mercifully given us a book which is 'able to make us wise unto salvation through faith in Christ Jesus' (2 Tim. 3:15). By reading that book we may learn what to believe, what to be, and what to do; how to live with comfort, and how to die in peace.

Practical Religion, 91.

Men may tell you there are difficulties in the Bible;—things hard to be understood. It would not be God's book if there were not. And what if there are? You do not despise medicines because you cannot explain all that your doctor does by them. But whatever men may say, the things needful to salvation are as clear as daylight. Be very sure of this,—people never reject the Bible because they cannot understand it. They understand it only too well; they understand that it condemns their own behaviour; they understand that it witnesses against their own sins, and summons them to judgment.

Thoughts for Young Men, 32.

I am afraid that the Bible of many a man and woman in Great Britain is *never read at all*. In one house that lies in a corner, stiff, cold, glossy, and fresh as it was when it came from the bookseller's shop. In another it lies on a table, with its owner's name written in it, a silent witness against him day after day.

Charges and Addresses, 353.

Neglect of the Bible is like disease of the body. It shows itself in the face of a man's conduct.

Charges and Addresses, 354.

Authority of the Bible

Let the Bible, the whole Bible, and nothing but the Bible, be the rule of our faith and practice. Holding this principle we travel upon the king's highway. The road may sometimes seem narrow, and our faith may be sorely tried, but we shall not be allowed greatly to err.— Departing from this principle we enter on a pathless wilderness. There is no telling what we may be led to believe or do. For ever let us bear this in mind. Here let us cast anchor. Here let us abide. It matters nothing who says a thing in religion, whether an ancient Father, or a modern bishop, or a learned divine. Is it in the Bible? Can it be proved by the Bible? If not, it is not to be believed.—It matters nothing how beautiful and clever sermons or religious books may appear. Are they in the smallest degree contrary to Scripture? If they are, they are rubbish and poison, and guides of no value.

Expository Thoughts on Luke, 1.283.

I can well understand an old divine saying, 'Give me a candle and a Bible, and shut me up in a dark dungeon, and I will tell you all that the whole world is doing.'

Practical Religion, 98.

Prove all things by the word of God;—all ministers, all teaching, all preaching, all doctrines, all sermons, all writings, all opinions, all practices,—prove all by the word of God.

Knots Untied, 51.

Higher Critics of the Bible

Let us regard all who would damage the authority of the Bible, or impugn its credit, as spiritual robbers.

We are travelling through a wilderness: they rob us of our only guide. We are voyaging over a stormy sea: they rob us of our only compass. We are toiling over a weary road: they pluck our staff out of our hands. And what do these spiritual robbers give us in place of the Bible? What do they offer as a safer guide and better provision for our souls? Nothing! Absolutely nothing! Big swelling words!

Empty promises of new light! High sounding jargon; but nothing substantial and real! They would fain take from us the bread of life, and they do not give us in its place so much as a stone.

Is All Scripture Inspired? 49.

I entirely repudiate the modern theory that the Pentateuch and its present form was never compiled till the times of Ezra and Nehemiah, and that many of the facts therein recorded, and especially in the first eleven chapters, are mere myths, fables, and legends, imagined or invented, and utterly destitute of solid and divine foundation. And if I am asked why I take up this ground, I answer, the theories I repudiate appear to me to *involve infinitely greater difficulties than the old traditional views* which I maintain.

Charges and Addresses, 292.

I cannot reconcile the views of modern Old Testament critics with the *use which our Lord Jesus Christ continually made* of the Old Testament scriptures in the Gospels, and with his mode of speaking about events, persons, and the things in the Pentateuch, and specially in the book of Genesis. This, after all, in my opinion, is the crucial test of the whole matter in dispute.

Charges and Addresses, 295.

Of course I do not forget that many 'Higher Critics' maintain that our Lord did not really believe in his own mind that Moses wrote the Pentateuch, or that the events narrated in Genesis actually took place. They say that, in order to avoid giving offense, he adopted the traditional views of his hearers, and accommodated himself to their ignorant legends. A more improbable solution of a difficulty I cannot conceive! If ever there was a teacher who was above flattering his hearers or accommodating his language to their prejudices, that teacher was our Lord.

Charges and Addresses, 297.

How to Read the Bible

For one thing, *begin reading your Bible this very day.*

Practical Religion, 122.

Read the Bible with childlike faith and humility. Open your heart as you open your book and say, 'Speak, Lord, for thy servant heareth.' Resolve to believe implicitly whatever you find there, however much it may run counter to your own prejudices. Resolve to receive heartily every statement of truth, whether you like it or not.

Practical Religion, 123.

Sit down to the study of it with a daily determination that *you* will live by it rules, rest on its statements, and act on its commands. Consider, as you travel through every chapter, 'How does this affect *my* position and course of conduct? What does this teach *me*? It is poor work to read the Bible from mere curiosity, and for speculative purposes, in order to fill your head and store your mind with opinions, while you do not allow the book to influence your heart and life. That Bible is read best which is practiced most.

Practical Religion, 123.

As one said quaintly, but most truly, 'Justification may be by faith, but a knowledge of the Bible comes only by works.'

Knots Untied, 66.

Inspiration of the Bible

If the Bible is not the word of God and inspired, the whole of Christendom for 1,800 years has been under an immense delusion; half the human race has been cheated and deceived, and churches are monuments of folly.

Is All Scripture Inspired? 3.

I abhor the 'mechanical' theory of inspiration. I dislike the idea that men like Moses and St Paul were no better than organ pipes, employed by the Holy Ghost, or ignorant secretaries or amanuenses who wrote by dictation what they did not understand. I admit nothing of the kind.

I believe that in some marvellous manner the Holy Ghost made use of the reason, the memory, the intellect, the style of thought, and the peculiar mental temperament of each writer of the Scriptures. But how and in what manner this was done I can no more explain than I can the union of two natures, God and man, in the person of our blessed Lord Jesus Christ. I only know that there is both a divine and a human element in the Bible and that, while the men who wrote it were really and truly men, the book that they wrote and handed down to us is really and truly the word of God. I know the *result*, but I do not understand the *process*.

Is All Scripture Inspired? 24-25.

The view which I maintain is that every book, and chapter, and verse, and syllable of the Bible was originally given by inspiration of God. I hold that not only the substance of the Bible, but its language,—not only the ideas of the Bible, but its words,—not only certain parts of the Bible, but every chapter of the book,—that all and each are of divine authority. I hold that the Scripture not only *contains* the Word of God, but *is* the Word of God.

Old Paths, 17-18.

If any man replies that the Holy Ghost did not *always* speak by Isaiah, I will ask him who is to decide when he did and when he did not? I see much in this.

Old Paths, 20.

Some object that there are things mentioned occasionally in the Bible which are so *trifling* that they are unworthy to be called inspired. They point to St Paul's writing about his cloak, and books, and parchments, and ask if we really think that the apostle wrote about such little matters by inspiration of God?—I answer that the least things affecting any of God's children are not too small for the notice of him who 'numbers the hairs of our heads.'

Old Paths, 23.

The Bible alone is absolutely perfect. From beginning to end it is 'the Word of God.'

Practical Religion, 93.

The exact manner in which the minds of the inspired writers of Scripture worked when they wrote, I do not pretend to explain. Very likely they could not have explained it themselves.

Is All Scripture Inspired? 24.

Stand fast in the old belief that the whole Bible from Genesis to Revelation was given by inspiration of God, and that the historical facts recorded in the Old Testament are all credible and true. Do not be shaken by vague assertions and big swelling words of those who sneer at everything supernatural, and talk about 'the laws of nature, the discoveries of science, and the results of modern criticism.'

Charges and Addresses, 227.

We must not expect to find, in a book inspired by the Spirit of God, no mysteries. We must rather remember that in nature there are many things we cannot understand; and that as it is in the book of nature, so it will always be in the book of revelation.

Knots Untied, 380.

Interpretation of the Bible

I hold it to be an infallible rule in the exposition of Scripture, that when two texts seem to contradict one another, the less plain must give way to the more plain, and the weak must give way to the strong. That doctrine which reconciles most texts of Scripture is most likely to be right. That doctrine which makes most texts quarrel with one another is most likely to be wrong.

Old Paths, 465.

The Holy Ghost made use of the reason, the memory, the intellect, the style of thought, and the peculiar mental temperament of each writer of the Scriptures. How and in what manner this was done, I can no more explain than I can the union of two natures, God and man, in the person of our blessed Lord Jesus Christ. I only know that there is both a divine and human element in the Bible and that, while the men who wrote it were really and truly men, the book that they wrote and handed down to us is really and truly the word of God. I know the result, but I do not understand the process.

Charges and Addresses, 239.

He that holds a Bible in his hand should remember that he holds not the word of man, but of God. He holds a volume which not *only contains, but is God's word.*

Charges and Addresses, 240.

Power of God's Word

Eighteen centuries have now passed away since God sent forth a few Jews from a remote corner of the earth, to do a work which according to man's judgment, must have seemed impossible. He sent them forth at a time when the whole world was full of superstition, cruelty, lust, and sin. He sent them forth to proclaim that the established religions of the earth were false and useless, and must be forsaken. He sent them forth to persuade men to give up old habits and customs, and to live different lives. He sent them forth to do battle with the most grovelling idolatry, with the vilest and most disgusting immorality, with vested interests, with old associations, with a bigoted priesthood, with sneering philosophers, with an ignorant population, with bloody-minded emperors, with the whole influence of Rome. Never was there an enterprise to all appearances more Quixotic and less likely to succeed!

And how did he arm them for this battle? He gave them no carnal weapons. He gave them no worldly power to compel assent, and no worldly riches to bribe belief. He simply put the Holy Ghost into their hearts, and the Scriptures into their hands.

Practical Religion, 99.

It is able to cleanse them, to sanctify them, to instruct them in righteousness, and to furnish them thoroughly for all good works (Psa. 119:9; John 17:17; 2 Tim. 3:16-17). The Spirit ordinarily does these things by the written Word; sometimes by the Word read, and sometimes by the Word preached, but seldom, if ever, without the Word.

Practical Religion, 105.

Science and the Bible

Remember that I have not the slightest sympathy with those weak-kneed Christians who seem to think that science and religion can never harmonize, and that they must always scowl and look askance at one another, like two quarrelsome dogs.

Charges and Addresses, 228.

Sufficiency of the Bible

'One plain text', said an old divine, 'is as good as a thousand reasons.'

Knots Untied, 32.

BISHOPS, CHURCH OF ENGLAND

A Bishop lives under the fierce blaze of public opinion; and he has always the sorrowful feeling that, whatever he may say or do, somebody or other is sure to be displeased.

Charges and Addresses, 37.

BLASPHEMY

The thoughts of some people about Christ are simply *blasphemous*. They are not ashamed to deny his divinity. They refuse to believe the miracles recorded of him. They pretend to find fault with not a few of his sayings and doings. They even question the perfect honesty and sincerity of some things that he did. They tell us that he ought to be ranked with great reformers and philosophers, like Socrates, Seneca, and Confucius, but no higher.

Christmas Thoughts, 38.

BOOK OF COMMON PRAYER

It is utterly untrue that the Prayer-book is a mere Popish book; considering that the greater part of it is pure Scripture. All these things are ridiculous untruths, which is a shame for any man to circulate, and a discredit to any man to believe.

Charges and Addresses, 54.

If all children are actually regenerated in baptism, because the Service says, 'this child is regenerate', then by parity of reasoning it follows that all people who use the Collect have faith, and a hearty desire to pray!—all women who are churched put their trust in the Lord!—all members of the Church who are buried are dear brethren, and we hope rest in Christ!—and all children who say the Catechism are sanctified by the Holy Ghost and our elect!—Consistency demands it. …

But if I am he told that the children who use the Catechism are not necessarily all elect and sanctified, and that the people buried are not necessarily all resting in Christ, and that the language in both cases is that of *charitable supposition*, then I reply, in common fairness let us be allowed to take the language of the Baptismal Service in the same sense.

Knots Untied, 159.

BORN AGAIN, REGENERATION

He only who breathed into Adam's nostrils the breath of life, can ever make a dead sinner a living Christian.

Old Paths, 128.

It is not merely reformation, or amendment, or moral change, or outward alteration of life. It is a thorough change of heart, will, and character. It is a resurrection. It is a new creation. It is a passing from death to life. It is the implanting in our dead hearts of a new principle from above. It is the calling into existence of a new creature, with a new nature, new habits of life, new tastes, new desires, new appetites, new judgments, new opinions, new hopes, and new fears. All this, and nothing less than this is implied, when our Lord declares that we all need a 'new birth.'

Expository Thoughts on John, 1.86.

No man is the author of his own existence, and no man can quicken his own soul. We might as well expect a dead man to give himself life, as expect a natural man to make himself spiritual.

Expository Thoughts on John, 1.86-87.

The change called the 'new birth,' our Lord would have us know, is of universal necessity. Nobody can be saved without it.

Expository Thoughts on John, 1.91.

He who knows best the time for people to be born, knows also the time for them to be born again.

Expository Thoughts on Luke, 1.10.

The natural birth is not a whit more necessary to the life of the body, than is the spiritual birth to the life of the soul (2 Cor. 5:17, John 3:3).

Old Paths, 121.

The most zealous efforts of ministers alone cannot make men Christians. The ablest scriptural reasoning has no effect on the mind; the most fervent pulpit eloquence will not move the heart; the naked truth alone will not lead the will. We who are ministers know this well by painful experience. We can show men the fountain of living waters, but we cannot make them drink. We see many a one sitting under our pulpits year after year, and hearing hundreds of sermons, full of gospel truth, without the slightest result. We mark him year after year, unaffected and unmoved by every scriptural argument,—cold as the stones on which he treads as he enters our church,—unmoved as the marble statue which adorns the tomb against the wall,—dead as the old dry oak of which his pew is made,—feelingless as the painted glass in the windows, through which the sun shines on his head. We look at him with wonder and sorrow, and remember Xavier's words as he looked at China: 'Oh, rock, rock! when wilt thou open?' And we learn by such cases as these, that nothing will make a Christian but the introduction into the heart of a new nature, a new principle, and a divine seed from above.

Old Paths, 255.

The love of sin must be taken from us, as well as the guilt of sin removed; the desire of pleasing God must be implanted in us, as well as the fear of God's judgment taken away; a love to holiness, must be engrafted, as well as a dread of punishment removed. Heaven itself would be no heaven to us if we entered it without a new heart.

Old Paths, 257.

The clearest head-knowledge will save no man. The most correct and orthodox views will not prevent a man perishing by the side of the most ignorant heathen, if he is not born again.

Old Paths, 480.

You may be born in the godliest family in the land, and enjoy the richest means of grace a church can supply, and yet never belong to the family of God. To belong to it you must be born again. None but the Holy Ghost can make a living member of his family.

Christmas Thoughts, 55.

The change required is not that of the snake when he casts his skin and yet remains a reptile still: it is the change of the caterpillar when he dies, and his crawling life ceases; but from the body rises the butterfly,—a new animal, with a new nature.

Knots Untied, 136.

A regenerate man *does not make the world's opinion his rule, of right and wrong.*

Knots Untied, 141.

Evidence of New Birth

Can any marks of the new birth be seen in us? Can the sound of the Spirit be heard in our daily conversation?

Expository Thoughts on John, 1.88.

A regeneration which produces no effects, bears no fruit, and cannot be seen in a person's life, is a regeneration never mentioned in Scripture.

Upper Room, 304.

Work of the Triune God

Sometimes the change is ascribed to God the Father: 'The God and Father of our Lord Jesus Christ … hath begotten us again unto a lively hope' (1 Pet. 1:3). Sometimes it is ascribed to God the Son: 'The Son quickeneth whom he will' (John 5:21). 'If ye know that he is righteous, ye know that every one that doeth righteousness is born of him' (1 John 2:29). Sometimes it is ascribed to the Spirit,—and he in fact is the great agent by whom it is always effected: 'That which is born of the Spirit is spirit' (John 3:6). But man has no power to work the change.

Knots Untied, 128.

CHARITY

Charity is rightly called 'the Queen of Christian graces.'

Practical Religion, 155.

CHILDREN

The eye of the child drinks in far more than the ear. A child will always observe what you do much more than what you say.

Holiness, 214.

'A wise son maketh a glad father' (Prov. 10:1). Whatever we seek for our sons and daughters, let us first seek that they may have a place in the covenant, and a name in the book of life.

Expository Thoughts on Luke, 1.10.

Remember children are born with a decided bias towards evil, and therefore if you let them choose for themselves, they are certain to choose wrong.

Upper Room, 245.

Parents, if you love your children, do all that lies in your power to train them up to a habit of prayer. Show them how to begin. Tell them what to say. Encourage them to persevere.

Upper Room, 253.

You will see many in this day who allow their children to choose and think for themselves long before they are able, and even make excuses for their disobedience, as if it were a thing not to be blamed. To my eyes, a parent always yielding, and a child always having its own way, are a most painful sight;—painful, because I see God's appointed order of things inverted and turned upside down;—painful, because I feel sure the consequence to that child's character in the end will be self-will, pride, and self-conceit. You must not wonder that men refuse to obey their Father which is in heaven, if you allow them, when children, to disobey their father who is upon earth.

Upper Room, 260.

Take care, then, what you do before a child. It is a true proverb, 'Who sins before a child, sins double.' Strive rather to be a living epistle of Christ, such as your families can read, and that plainly too.

Upper Room, 269.

Children require no schooling to learn to sin.

Upper Room, 270.

Children in Church

Tell them of the duty and privilege of going to the house of God, and joining in the prayers of the congregation. Tell them that wherever the Lord's people are gathered together, there the Lord Jesus is present in an especial manner, and that those who absent themselves must expect, like the Apostle Thomas, to miss a blessing.

Upper Room, 254.

I call it a sad sight in a church when nobody comes up to the Lord's table but the elderly people, and the young men and the young women all turn away. But I call it a sadder sight still when no children are to be seen in a church, excepting those who come to the Sunday School, and are obliged to attend.

Upper Room, 255.

Disciplining Children

As to the best way of punishing a child, no general rule can be laid down. The characters of children are so exceedingly different, that what would be a severe punishment to one child, would be no punishment at all to another.

Upper Room, 265, fn. 2.

Teaching Children

He [God] gives your children a mind that will receive impressions like moist clay. He gives them a disposition at the starting point of life to believe what you tell them, and to take for granted what you advise them, and to trust your word rather than a stranger's. He gives you, in short, a golden opportunity of doing them good. See that the opportunity be not neglected, and thrown away.

Upper Room, 248.

He that has trained his children for heaven, rather than for earth,—for God, rather than for man,—he is the parent that will be called wise at last.

Upper Room, 250.

CHRISTIAN

To talk of God being men's Father, and men being God's children, while they do not believe on the Son of God, is contrary to Scripture. Those are not children of God who have not faith in Jesus.

Expository Thoughts on John, 1.15.

To be a Christian it will cost a man the favour of the world.

Holiness, 98.

He has a portion that will never be taken from him, a Saviour that will never be taken from him, a Saviour that will never forsake him, a treasure that fadeth not away, however little he may realize it all at present.

Holiness, 164.

The professing Christian has the best of leaders: Jesus the Captain of Salvation, through whom he may be more than conqueror—the best of provisions, the bread and water of life—and the best of pay promised to him: an eternal weight of glory.

Holiness, 314.

Let it not be our distinctive character that we are men of science—or men of literary attainments—or men of the world—or men of pleasure, or men of business—but 'men of God.'

Holiness, 319.

We have been baptized with water. But have we also been baptized with the Holy Ghost?—Our names are in the baptismal register. But are they also in the Lamb's book of life?—We are members of the visible church. But are we also members of that mystical body of which Christ alone is the Head?—All these are privileges which Christ alone bestows, and for which all who would be saved must make personal application to him. Man cannot give them. They are treasures laid up in Christ's hand. From him we must seek them by faith and prayer, and believing we shall not seek in vain.

Expository Thoughts on Luke, 1.75.

Once he cared only for this world, its pleasures, its business, its occupations, its rewards. Now he looks upon it as an empty, unsatisfying place,—an inn,—a lodging,—a training-school for the life to come. His treasure is in heaven. His home is beyond the grave.

Old Paths, 125.

The heart is the seat of true religion, and the true Christian is the Christian in heart.

Practical Religion, 246.

Pardon, peace, hope, guidance, comfort, consolation, grace according to your need, strength according to your day, joy which the world can neither give nor take away,—all this I can boldly promise to the man who comes to Christ, and serves him with his heart. But I cannot promise him that his religion will be popular with man. I would rather warn him to expect mockery and ridicule, slander and unkindness, opposition and persecution. There is a cross belonging to heart-religion, and we must be content to carry it.

Practical Religion, 262-63.

True Christians, above all, are called 'a family' because there is so strong a *family likeness* among them. They are all led by one Spirit, and are marked by the same general features of life, heart, taste, and character. Just as there is a general bodily resemblance among the brothers and sisters of family, so there is a general spiritual resemblance among all the sons and daughters of the Lord Almighty. They all hate sin and love God. They all rest their hope of salvation on Christ, and have no confidence in themselves. They all endeavour to come out and be separate from the ways of the world, and to set their affections on things above. They all turn naturally to the same Bible as the only food of their souls, and the only sure guide in their pilgrimage toward heaven. They find it a 'lamp to their feet, and a light to their path' (Psa. 119:105). They all go to the same throne of grace in prayer, and find it as needful to speak to God as to breathe.

Christmas Thoughts, 57-58.

They live in the midst of an evil world, and are often sick of themselves and of the sin they see around them.

Christmas Thoughts, 63.

The path of the worldly man grows darker and darker every year that he lives;—the path of the Christian is as a shining light, brighter and brighter to the very end. His sun is just rising when the sun of the worldly is setting for ever;—his best things are all beginning to blossom and bloom for ever, when those of the worldly are all slipping out of his hands, and passing away.

Thoughts for Young Men, 75.

Benefits of Christians

Is he laden with many sins? Though they be as scarlet they shall be white as snow.

Is his heart hard and prone to evil? A new heart shall be given to him, and a new spirit put in him.

Is he weak and cowardly? He that enabled Peter to confess Christ before his enemies shall make him bold.

Is he ignorant? He that bore with Thomas' slowness shall bear with him, and guide him into all truth.

Is he alone in his position? He that stood by Paul when all men forsook him shall also stand by his side.

Practical Religion, 306.

Christian Character

The grace of God in conversion does not so re-mould a man as to leave no trace of his natural bent of character. The sanguine do not altogether cease to be sanguine, nor the desponding to be desponding, when they pass from death to life, and become true Christians. They show us that we must make large allowances for natural temperament, in forming our estimate of individual Christians.

Expository Thoughts on John, 2.179
(also *Power and Sympathy of Christ,* 29).

Live like one who thoroughly believes that time is short and eternity near, the devil strong, and sin abounding,—the darkness very great and the light very small,—the ungodly very many and the godly very few,—the things of the world mere transitory shadows, and heaven and hell the great substantial realities.

Old Paths, 86.

It ought not to be necessary to tell people, as in the case of a badly painted picture, 'This is a Christian.'

Old Paths, 137.

We may fall short, but let us aim high.

Old Paths, 196.

Many are the bitter things which people write against themselves, by expecting to find in their hearts what cannot be found on this side of heaven. Let us settle it in our minds that saints on earth are not perfect angels, but only converted sinners.

Expository Thoughts on John, 2.186
(also *Power and Sympathy of Christ,* 45).

Doubting Believers

I do not shrink from saying that by grace a man may have sufficient faith to flee to Christ; sufficient faith really to lay hold on him—really to trust in him—really to be a child of God—really to be saved; and yet to his last day be never free from much anxiety, doubt, and fear.

Holiness, 145.

Too many among those who believe begin doubting and go on doubting, live doubting and die doubting, and go to heaven in a kind of mist.

Holiness, 148.

Spiritual darkness comes on horseback, and goes away on foot.

Holiness, 167.

Let us cleave to Christ more closely, love him more heartily, live to him more thoroughly, copy him more exactly, confess him more boldly, follow him more fully.

Practical Religion, 349.

False Professors

The very fact that there are many false professors in the churches is an indirect proof that there are such persons as true-hearted and sound believers.

Upper Room, 183.

Spiritual Warfare of the Christian

There must be constant *watchfulness* against the enemies of your soul. He that would have peace must be always prepared for war.

Old Paths, 222.

CHRISTIANITY

True Christianity is not merely the believing a certain set of dry abstract propositions: it is to live in daily personal communication with an actual living person—Jesus, the Son of God.

Practical Religion, 330.

Justification by faith and sanctification of the heart ... are the grand essentials of the Christian religion. These are no mere words and names to furnish bones of contention for wrangling theologians.

Practical Religion, 342.

The whole power of imperial Rome, with her legions, proved unable to stamp out the religion which began with a few fishermen and publicans in Palestine. They overcame by FAITH.

Upper Room, 124.

Weak Christianity

It may be that a certain profession of religion has become so fashionable and comparatively easy in the present age, that the streams which were once narrow and deep have become wide and shallow, and what we have gained in outward show we have lost in quality.

Holiness, 17.

I can find no words to express my deep sense of the importance of maintaining in our church the true doctrine of the blood of Christ. One plague of our age is the widespread dislike to what men are pleased to call dogmatic theology. In the place of it, the idol of the day is a kind of jellyfish Christianity,—a Christianity without bone, or muscle, or sinew—without any distinct teaching about the atonement or the work of the Spirit, or justification, or the way of peace with God—a vague, foggy, misty Christianity, of which the only watchwords seem to be, 'You must be earnest, and real, and true, and brave, and zealous, and liberal, and kind. You must condemn no man's doctrinal views. You must consider everybody is right, and nobody is wrong.' And this creedless kind of religion, we are actually told, is to give us peace of conscience!

Upper Room, 80.

CHRISTMAS

How many, in their Christmas plans and arrangements, give a thought to him, without whom there would have been no Christmas at all?

Christmas Thoughts, 32.

CHURCH

The true glory of a church does not consist in its buildings for public worship, but in the faith and godliness of its members.

Expository Thoughts on Mark, 215.

Let it be a settled principle in our religion, however beautiful we make our churches, to regard pure doctrine and holy practice as their principal ornaments. *Without* these two things, the noblest ecclesiastical edifice is radically defective. It has no glory if God is not there.

Expository Thoughts on Mark, 216.

Statesmen, rulers, emperors, kings, presidents, heads of governments, have their schemes and plans, and think them of vast importance. But there is another work going on of infinitely greater moment, for which they are only the 'axes and saws' in God's hands

(Isa. 10:15). That work is the erection of Christ's spiritual temple, the gathering in of living stones into the one true church.

Holiness, 292-93.

No doubt there is plenty of hypocrisy and false profession in the churches; no doubt there are thousands whose religious feelings are mere delusion. But bad money is no proof that there is no such thing as good coin: the abuse of a thing does not destroy the use of it.

Old Paths, 262.

There is a Judas Iscariot at every communion table, and a Demas in every apostolic company; and wherever the sons of God come together, Satan is sure to appear among them.

Christmas Thoughts, 108-9.

A Church, like every other corporation on earth, must have definite terms of membership. It must have a creed, and certain fixed principles of doctrine and worship. Its members have a right to know what its ministers are set to teach.

Charges and Addresses, 34, 383.

Church Buildings

By all means let us have handsome churches, if we can get them, but let us not waste money on bricks and mortar, especially in poor districts. For another thing, I entreat the promoters of new churches to beware of opening them with a heavy debt on them. Nothing, I am certain, so paralyses the minister of a new church as the incessant struggle to pay off a debt. It is like a mill-stone around his neck, and seriously cripples his usefulness, at that critical period, the beginning of his work.

Charges and Addresses, 143.

The humblest cottage-meeting, where Christ is preached, and the Scriptures honoured, and a few real believers are assembled, is more pleasing in his sight than the grandest cathedral in which the Gospel is never heard, and no work of the Spirit ever goes on.

Charges and Addresses, 202-3.

Church Divisions

At the end of eighteen centuries we all know, by bitter experience, that the divisions of Christians are the weakness of the church, and the favourite argument of the world, the infidel, and the devil against revealed religion.

Upper Room, 6.

There are some handwritings on the wall which it needs no Daniel to interpret, and I heartily wish all loyal Churchmen would awake and look at them. A house divided against itself cannot stand.

Charges and Addresses, 224.

I believe that it is miserable policy to try to purchase unity and peace and charity at the expense of faith and hope and truth.

Charges and Addresses, 385.

Beware of divisions. One thing the children of the world can always understand if they do not understand doctrine. That thing is angry quarrelling and controversy. Be at peace among yourselves.

Charges and Addresses, 424.

Church Leadership and Laity

Above all, we want a Council in which bishops, presbyters, and laymen, shall sit together and consider subjects face to face. The clergy would then have an opportunity of finding out what public opinion is, and discovering that they are not infallible.

Upper Room, 296.

Church Membership

Tell me not that you have been baptized and taught the catechism of the Church of England, and therefore must be a child of God. I tell you that the parish register is not the book of life.

Practical Religion, 392.

Duties of Members

The man who thinks that the office of churchwarden completely fulfils the New Testament idea of the laity's position in a church must have taken leave of his common sense.

Upper Room, 284.

The vast majority of church-goers appear to suppose that when they have gone to church on Sunday, and have been at the Lord's Supper, they have done their duty, and are not under the slightest obligation to warn, to teach, to rebuke, to edify others, to promote works of charity, to assist evangelization, or to raise a finger in checking sin, and advancing Christ's cause in the world. Their only idea is to be perpetually receiving, but never doing anything at all. They have taken their seats in the right train, and are only to sit quiet, while the clerical engine draws them to heaven, perhaps half asleep. If an Ephesian or Philippian or Thessalonian lay Churchman were to rise from the dead and see how little work lay Churchmen do for the English Church, he would not believe his eyes.

Upper Room, 285.

Encourage and invite every right-minded layman near you to come forward and give you his help. Never, never be afraid of enlisting the aid of the laity. Cast away forever the old tradition that religious work is to be left to the clergy alone.

Charges and Addresses, 42.

A praying, interceding people are the very backbone of a Church.

Charges and Addresses, 137.

We may depend on it, an increase of practical godliness is the only sure test of a Church's health and prosperity.

Charges and Addresses, 374.

Let us never make ministers popes. Let us follow them so far as they follow Christ, but not a hair's breadth further.

Knots Untied, 55.

False Churches

There are many places of worship, I fear, where you might look long for Christ crucified, and never find him. He is buried under outward ceremonies,—thrust behind the baptismal font,—lost sight of under the shadow of the church. 'They have taken away my Lord, and I know not where they have laid him' (John 20:13). Take heed where you settle yourself. Try all by this single test, 'Is Jesus and free forgiveness proclaimed here?' There may be comfortable pews, —there may be good singing, there may be learned sermons. But if Christ's gospel is not the sun and centre of the whole place, do not pitch your tent there. Say rather with Isaac, 'Here, is the wood and the fire, but where is the lamb?' (Gen. 22:7). Be very sure this is not the place for your soul.

Old Paths, 181.

A Church which does not honour the Bible is as useless as a body without life, or a steam engine without fire. A minister who does not honour the Bible is as useless as a soldier without arms, a builder without tools, a pilot without compass, or a messenger without tidings.

Light from Old Times, 8-9.

Invisible Church

The life of its members does not hang on church membership and baptism and the Lord Supper, although they highly value these things, when they are to be had. But it has only one great Head,—one Shepherd,—one chief Bishop,—and that is Jesus Christ. He alone, by his Spirit, admits the members of this church, though the ministers may show the door. Till he opens the door, no man on earth can open it,—neither bishops, nor presbyters, nor convocations, nor synods. Once let a man repent and believe the gospel, and that moment he becomes a member of this church.

Knots Untied, 242.

Visible Church

In short, the visible church of Christ may be divided into two great parties, those who 'minister' to Christ, and those who do not.

Expository Thoughts on Luke, 1.189.

The best visible church of Christ is not free from a liability to degenerate. It is made up of fallible men. There is always in it a tendency to leave its first love.

Knots Untied, 61.

CHURCH GOVERNMENT

There is not a text in the Bible which expressly commands churches to have one special form of government, and expressly forbids any other. If there is, let men point it out. There is not a text which expressly confines Christians to the use of a Liturgy, or expressly enjoins them only to have extempore prayer. If there is, let it be shown. And yet for hundreds of years Episcopalians and Presbyterians and Independents have contended with each other, as if these things had been settled as minutely as the Levitical ceremonies, and as if everybody who did not see with their eyes was almost guilty of a deadly sin!

Knots Untied, 251.

CHURCH OF ENGLAND

I have long maintained, and still maintain, that every well-constituted National Church ought to be as comprehensive as possible. It should allow large liberty of thought within certain limits. Its '*necessaria*' or should be few and well-defined. Its '*non-necessaria*' should be very many. It should make generous allowance for the infinite variety of men's minds, the curious sensitiveness of scrupulous consciences, and the enormous difficulty of clothing thoughts in language which will not admit of more than one meaning. A sect can afford to be narrow and exclusive: a National Church ought to be liberal, generous, and as 'large-hearted' as Solomon (1 Kings 4:29). Above all, the rulers of such a Church should never forget that it is a body of which the members, from the highest minister down to the humblest layman, are all fallen and corrupt creatures, and that their mental errors, as well as their moral delinquencies, demand very tender dealing.

Charges and Addresses, 32.

CONFESSING CHRIST

Our Lord declares, that if we do not confess him before men, he will 'not confess us before the angels of God' at the last day. He will refuse to acknowledge us as his people. He will disown us as cowards, faithless, and deserters. He will not plead for us. He will not be our Advocate. He will not deliver us from the wrath to come. He will leave us to reap the consequences of our cowardice, and to stand before the bar of God helpless, defenceless, and unforgiven.

Expository Thoughts on Luke, 2.49.

COMPASSION

Sympathy is not sinful, but Christlike.

Expository Thoughts on John, 2.200
(also *Power and Sympathy of Christ*, 76).

COMPLAINING

It is no mark of a healthy state of soul when there is much complaining and little praise.

Practical Religion, 27.

Fault-finding is the easiest of all tasks.

Knots Untied, 266.

CONSCIENCE

There is only one thing can give peace to the conscience, and that is the blood of Jesus Christ sprinkled on it. A clear understanding that Christ's death was an actual payment of our debt to God, and that the merit of that death is made over to man when he believes, is the grand secret of inward peace.

Christmas Thoughts, 90.

His conscience, I think, will tell him, if he will let it speak, that God is perfect, and he imperfect; that God is very high, and he very low; that God is glorious majesty and he a poor worm; and that if ever he is to stand before him in judgment with comfort, then he must have some mighty Helper, or he will not be saved.

Knots Untied, 36.

CONVERSION

All true Christians are led by one Spirit, washed in one blood, serve one Lord, lean on one Saviour, believe one truth, and walk by one general rule. But all are not converted in one and the same manner. All do not pass through the same experience. In conversion, the Holy Spirit acts as a sovereign. He calls everyone severally as he will.

Expository Thoughts on John, 1.55.

Nothing can happen to a man which ought to be such an occasion of joy, as his conversion. It is a far more important event than being married, or coming of age, or being made a nobleman, or receiving a great fortune. It is the birth of an immortal soul! It is the rescue of a sinner from hell! It is a passage from life to death! It is being made a king and priest for evermore! It is being provided for, both in time and eternity! It is adoption into the noblest and richest of all families, the family of God!

Expository Thoughts on Luke, 1.114-15.

There is no sinner too far gone in sin for Christ to raise and convert. He that stood by the grave of Lazarus can say to the vilest of men, 'Come forth: loose him, and let him go.'

Expository Thoughts on John, 2.205
(also *Power and Sympathy of Christ,* 86).

I believe that just as 'no man liveth unto himself' (Rom. 14:7), so also no man is converted only for himself; and that the conversion of one man or woman always leads on, in God's wonderful providence, to the conversion of others.

Upper Room, 105.

Conversions may not be in your time, and you may die without seeing them. But never doubt that conversion generally leads to conversions, and that few go to heaven alone. When [William] Grimshaw, of Haworth, the 'apostle of the north,' died, he left his son graceless and godless. Afterwards the son was converted, never having forgotten his father's advice and example. And his last words were, 'What will my old father say when he sees me in heaven?'

Upper Room, 107.

Evidences of Conversion

Does anyone ask me what we may expect to see in a true conversion? I reply, There will always be something seen in a converted man's character, and feelings, and conduct, and opinions, and daily life. You will not see in him perfection; but you will see in him something peculiar, distinct, and different from other people. You will see him hating sin, loving Christ, following after holiness, taking pleasure in his Bible, persevering in prayer. You will see him penitent, humble, believing, temperate, charitable, truthful, good-tempered, patient, upright, honourable, kind. These, at any rate, will be his aims: these are the things which he will follow after, however short he may come of perfection.

Old Paths, 315.

False Conversion

Not a few are ready to pronounce any change for the better in a man's character, a conversion. They forget that there may be many blossoms on a tree in spring, and yet no fruit in autumn, and that a new coat of paint does not make an old door new.

Old Paths, 469.

COVENANT

He is the eternal Son of God, whom the Father loved from all eternity, and into whose hands all things concerning man's salvation have been given and committed by an everlasting covenant.

Expository Thoughts on John, 1.131.

We can understand what a covenant is between man and man. It is an agreement between two persons, by which they bind themselves to fulfil certain conditions and do certain things. But who can fully understand a covenant made by the Eternal God?

Upper Room, 222.

Covenant of Redemption

It is a mysterious and ineffable arrangement whereby all things necessary for the salvation of our souls, our present peace, and our final glory, are fully and completely provided, and all this by the joint work of God the Father, God the Son, and God the Holy Ghost. The redeeming work of God the Son by dying as our substitute on the cross,—the drawing work of God the Father by choosing and drawing us to the Son,—and the sanctifying work of the Holy Ghost in awakening, quickening, and renewing our fallen nature,—are all contained in this covenant, besides everything that the soul of the believer needs between grace and glory.

Upper Room, 223.

Our names have long been in the Lamb's book of life. Our pardon and peace of conscience through Christ's blood, our strength for duty, our comfort in trial, our power to fight Christ's battles, were all arranged for us from endless ages, and long before we were born.

Upper Room, 223.

It is recorded of Bernard Gilpin, a Reformer who lived in the days of the Marian martyrdoms, and was called the Apostle of the North, that he was famous for never murmuring or complaining, whatever happened to him. In the worst and blackest times he used to be always saying, 'It is all in God's everlasting covenant, and must be for good.' Towards the close of Queen Mary's reign, he was suddenly summoned to come up from Durham to London, to be tried for heresy, and in all probability, like Ridley and Latimer, to be burned. The good man quietly obeyed the summons, and said to his mourning friends, 'It is in the covenant, and must be for good.' On his journey from Durham to London, his horse fell, and his leg was broken, and he was laid up at a roadside inn. Once more he was asked, 'What do you think of this?' Again he replied, 'It is all in the covenant, and must be for good.' And so it turned out. Weeks and weeks passed away before his leg was healed, and he was able to resume his journey. But during those weeks the unhappy Queen Mary died, the persecutions were stopped, and the worthy old Reformer returned to his northern home rejoicing. 'Did I not tell you,' he said to his friends, 'that all was working together for good?'

Upper Room, 225.

COVETOUSNESS

It was this sin which helped to cast down the angels who fell. They were not content with their first estate. They coveted something better. It was this sin which helped to drive Adam and Eve out of paradise, and bring death into the world. Our first parents were not satisfied with the things which God gave them in Eden. They coveted, and so they fell.—It is a sin which, ever since the fall, has been the fertile cause of misery and unhappiness upon earth. Wars, quarrels, strifes, divisions, envyings, disputes, jealousies, hatreds of all sorts, both public and private, may nearly all be traced up to this fountain-head.

Expository Thoughts on Luke, 2.54.

CROSS

The cross is the effect of the Father's love, and not the cause. Redemption is the result of the compassion of all three Persons in the Trinity. To place the Father and the Son in opposition one to another, is weak and crude theology. Christ died, not because God the Father hated, but because he loved the world.

Old Paths, 356.

No man ever perished and went to hell from the foot of the cross. If you can do nothing else, lie down at the foot of the cross.

Old Paths, 375.

DEATH

The first grave that ever was dug on this earth, was that of a young man: the first person who ever died, was not a father but a son. … He that is wise will never reckon confidently on long life.

Expository Thoughts on John, 1.178.

All is not over when men die.

Expository Thoughts on John, 1.206.

You cannot live always: there must be an end one day. The last sermon will one day be heard; the last prayer will one day be prayed; the last chapter in the Bible will one day be read—meaning, wishing, hoping, intending, resolving, doubting, hesitating—all will at length be over. You will have to leave this world and to stand before a holy God.

Holiness, 238.

Death himself shall die.

Expository Thoughts on Luke, 2.253.

Men like Paine and Voltaire have often shown that their vaunted philosophy breaks down when the grave is in sight. Tell me not what a man thinks about the soul when he is in the fullness of health; tell me rather what he thinks when the world is sinking beneath him, and death, judgment, and eternity loom in sight.

Old Paths, 49.

Time is short, and is passing quickly away: yet a few years, and we shall be all dead and gone. The trees perhaps are cut down out of which our coffins will be made: the winding-sheets perhaps are woven which will surround our bodies; the spades perhaps are made that will dig our graves. Eternity draws near. There ought to be no trifling. 'What, what is your hope about your soul?'.

Old Paths, 104.

One dying thief was saved that men might not despair, but only one that none might presume.

Practical Religion, 345.

Death himself shall one day die (Rev. 20:14).

Practical Religion, 350.

Death locks the door on the unbeliever, and shuts him out from hope. But death opens the door to the believer, and lets him into Paradise.

Practical Religion, 426.

It matters little where we die. All graves are equally near to Paradise. But it does matter much whether we belong to God's family.

Christmas Thoughts, 69.

Let us note here what a humbling lesson death teaches. So terrible and painful is the corruption of a body, when the breath leaves it, that even those who love us most are glad to bury us out of sight (Gen. 23:4).

Expository Thoughts on John, 2.207
(also *Power and Sympathy of Christ,* 90).

Homer, and Plato, and Bolingbroke, and Voltaire, and Paine are all alike cheerless and silent when they look down into an open grave.

Upper Room, 51.

What can take the sting of death away?—There is but one answer to such questions. Nothing but strong faith can do it. Faith laying firm hold on an unseen Saviour,—faith resting on the promises of an unseen God,—faith, and faith only, can enable a man to look death in the face, and say, 'I depart in peace.'

Expository Thoughts on Luke, 1.52.

Look at the churchyards and cemeteries. One by one the people around you are dropping into them, and you must lie there one day.

Practical Religion, 18.

The history of Marlborough, and Washington, and Napoleon, and Wellington, arrive at just the same humbling conclusion. The end of each, after all his greatness is just this,—'he died.'

Practical Religion, 303.

Death and Resurrection of Christians

The very moment that believers die they are in paradise. Their battle is fought: their strife is over. They have passed through that gloomy valley we must one day tread; they have gone over that dark river we must one day cross. They have drunk that last bitter cup which sin has mingled for man: they have reached that place where sorrow and sighing are no more. Surely we should not wish them back again!

Holiness, 258.

The Christian believer is the only one who can truly regard death as sleep,—that is, as a healthy, refreshing thing, which can do him no harm. Many among ourselves, perhaps, are not aware that the figure of speech exists among us in full force in the word 'cemetery,' applied to burial ground. That word is drawn from the very Greek verb which our Lord uses here. It is literally a 'sleeping place.'

Expository Thoughts on John, 2.182
(also *Power and Sympathy of Christ,* 35).

When they go down the valley of the shadow of death, and friends and relatives stand still and can go no further, he goes down by their side. When they wake up in the unknown world of Paradise, they are still with him; when they rise with a new body at the judgment day, they will not be alone. He will own them for his friends, and say, 'They are mine: deliver them and let them go free.' He will make good his own words: 'I am with you always, even unto the end of the world' (Matt. 28:20).

Practical Religion, 328.

Dead in Sin

We may change our sins, but we cannot change our hearts.

Old Paths, 127.

What should you have said, if you had seen Joseph weeping over his father Jacob?—'He fell upon his face, and wept upon him, and kissed him' (Gen. 50:1). But there was no reply to his affection. All about that aged countenance was unmoved, silent, and still. Doubtless you would have guessed the reason.—Jacob was dead.

What would you have said, if you had heard the Levite speaking to his wife, when he found her lying before the door in Gibeah? 'Up', he said, 'and let us be going. But none answered' (Judg. 19:28). His words were thrown away. There she lay, motionless, stiff, and cold. You know the cause.—She was dead.

What should you have thought, if you had seen the Amalekite stripping Saul of his royal ornaments in Mount Gilboa? He 'took from him the crown that was upon his head, and the bracelet that was on his arm' (2 Sam. 1:10). There was no resistance. Not a muscle moved in that proud face: not a finger was raised to prevent him. And why?—Saul was dead.

What should you have thought, if you had met the widow's son in the gate of Nain, lying on a bier, wrapped about with grave-clothes, followed by his weeping mother, carried slowly towards the tomb? (Luke 7:12). Doubtless it would have been all clear to you. It would have needed no explanation.—The young man was dead.

Now I say this is just the condition of every man by nature in the matter of his soul. I say this is just the state of the vast majority of people around us in spiritual things.

Old Paths, 116-17.

The poet's words are strictly true,—

> He only lives who lives to God,
> And all are dead beside.

This is the true explanation of sin not felt,—and sermons not believed,—and good advice not followed,—and the gospel not embraced,—and the world not forsaken,—and the cross not taken up,—and self-will not mortified,—and evil habits not laid aside,—and the Bible seldom read,—and the knee never bent in prayer. Why is all this on every side? The answer is simple: *Men are dead.*

Old Paths, 118.

Naturally we should never choose the things which are for our peace; we should never come to Christ. Whatever be our rank in life, our *affections* need to be turned to things above:—naturally we only set them on things below, earthly, sensual, short lived, and vain. Pride must give place to humility,—self-righteousness to self-abasement,—carelessness to seriousness,—worldliness to holiness,—unbelief to faith. Satan's dominion must be put down within us, and the kingdom of God set up. Self must be crucified, and Christ must reign. Till these things come to pass, we are dead as stones. When these things begin to take place, and not till then, we are *alive.*

Old Paths, 123.

DISAGREEMENTS

We must make up our minds to see differences … among Christians so long as the world stands. We may regret them much, because of the handle they give to an ignorant and prejudiced world. But they will exist, and are one of the many evidences of our fallen condition. About church government, about the manner of conducting public worship, about fasts and feasts, and saint's days, and ceremonials, Christians have never been entirely of one mind, even from the days of the apostles. On all these points the holiest and ablest servants of God have arrived at different conclusions. Argument, reasoning, persuasion, persecution, have all alike proved unable to produce unity.

Expository Thoughts on Luke, 1.118

DISCIPLESHIP

Though led by different paths, they all entered the same road, embraced the same truths, served the same Master, and at length reached the same home.

Expository Thoughts on John, 1.55.

DISOBEDIENCE

One Achan allowed in the camp of your heart will weaken your hands and lay your consolations low in the dust.

Holiness, 162.

DIVISION

In too many English parishes, both in town and country, true love seems almost dead, both in church and chapel, and wretched party spirit and controversy are the only fruits that Christianity appears able to produce.

Practical Religion, 14.

DOCTRINE

For your own soul's sake, dare to make up your mind what you believe, and dare to have positive, distinct views of truth and error. Never, never be afraid to hold decided doctrinal opinions; and let no fear of man and no morbid dread of being thought party-spirited, narrow, or controversial, make you rest contented with a bloodless, boneless, tasteless, colourless, lukewarm, undogmatic Christianity.

Holiness, 398.

I fear the increasing tendency to regard all doctrinal questions as matters of opinion, and to look on all 'earnest-minded' men as right, whatever doctrines they maintain. I warn you that the sure result of giving way to this tendency will be a vague, low, misty theology,—a theology containing no positive hope, no positive motive, and no positive consolation,—a theology which will fail most, just when it is most wanted, in the day of affliction, the hour of sickness, and on the bed of death.

Old Paths, 471-72.

Christianity without dogma is a powerless thing. It may be beautiful to some minds, but it is childless and barren.

Charges and Addresses, 65.

Apathy to Doctrine

I am afraid of an inward disease which appears to be growing and spreading in all the Churches of Christ throughout the world. That disease is a disposition on the part of ministers to abstain from all sharply-cut doctrine, and a distaste on the part of professing Christians for all distinct statements of dogmatic truth.

Charges and Addresses, 57.

We have hundreds of ministers, both inside and outside the Church of England, who seem not to have a single bone in their body of divinity. They have no definite opinions; they belong to no school or party; they are so afraid of 'extreme views,' that they have no views at all. We have thousands of sermons preached every year, which are without an edge or a point or a corner, smooth as ivory balls, awakening no sinner, and edifying no saint. We have legions of young men annually turned out from our Universities, armed with a few scraps of secondhand philosophy, who think it a mark of cleverness and intellect to have no decided opinions about anything in religion, and to be utterly unable to make up their minds as to what is Christian truth.

Charges and Addresses, 60-61.

EFFECTUAL CALL

Our Lord lays down the great principle 'that no man whatsoever can come to Christ by faith, and really believe in him, unless God the Father draws him so to come, and inclines his will to believe.' The nature of man since the fall is so corrupt and depraved, that even when Christ is made known and preached to him, he will not come to him and believe in him, without the special grace of God inclining his will and giving him a disposition to come. Moral suasion and advice alone will not bring him. He must be 'drawn.'

Expository Thoughts on John, 1.271.

It is a drawing which the Father effects through the man's own will by creating a new principle within him. By the unseen agency of the Holy Ghost he works on the man's heart, without the man himself knowing it at the time, inclines him to think, induces him to feel, shows him his sinfulness, and so leads him at length to Christ.

Expository Thoughts on John, 1.271.

ELECTION

The elect of God prove themselves to be elect by 'choosing' the things which are according to God's mind. The wicked prove themselves to be only fit for destruction, by 'choosing, loving, and following' the things which must lead to destruction.

Expository Thoughts on John, 1.117.

They are chosen in Christ from all eternity and then drawn to Christ in time.

Expository Thoughts on John, 1.272.

The true doctrine of election I believe to be as follows. God has been pleased from all eternity to choose certain men and women out of mankind, whom by his counsel secret to us, he has decreed to save by Jesus Christ. None are finally saved except those who are thus chosen.

Old Paths, 432.

None ever repent, believe, and are born again, except the elect. The primary and original cause of a saint's being what he is, is God's eternal election.

Old Paths, 432.

It is an old and quaint saying, but a very true one: 'A man must first go to the little Grammar-school of Repentance and Faith, before he enters the great University of Election and Predestination.'

Old Paths, 443.

Election and Sanctification

The Bible knows of no election except through 'sanctification,'—no eternal choosing except that we should be 'holy,'—no predestination except to be 'conformed to the image of God's Son'. When these things are lacking, it is mere waste of time to talk of election (1 Pet. 1:2; Eph. 1:4; Rom. 8:29).

Old Paths, 440.

ENDURANCE

(a) When Moses refused the pleasures of sin in Egypt, and chose affliction with the people of God—this was overcoming: he overcame the *love of pleasure.*

(b) When Micaiah refused to prophesy smooth things to King Ahab, though he knew he would be persecuted if he spoke the truth—this was overcoming: he overcame the *love of ease.*

(c) When Daniel refused to give up praying, though he knew the den of lions was prepared for him—this was overcoming: he overcame the *fear of death.*

(d) When Matthew rose from the receipt of custom at our Lord's bidding, left all and followed him—this was overcoming: he overcame the *love of money.*

(e) When Peter and John stood up boldly before the council and said, 'We cannot but speak the things we have seen and heard'—this was overcoming: they overcame the *fear of man.*

(f) When Saul the Pharisee gave up all his prospects of preferment among the Jews, and preached that very Jesus whom he had once persecuted—this was overcoming: he overcame the *love of man's praise.*

Holiness, 315.

ENVY

Envy not your wealthy neighbours: be content with such things as you have. Happiness does not depend on houses or land; silks and satins cannot shut out sorrow from the heart; castles and halls cannot prevent anxiety and care coming in at their doors.

Practical Religion, 232.

EQUALITY

Universal equality is a very high sounding expression, and a favourite idea with visionary men. Many in every age have disturbed society by stirring up the poor against the rich, and by preaching up the popular doctrine that all men ought to be equal. But so long as the world is under the present order of things this universal equality cannot be attained.

Practical Religion, 297.

Take all the property in England by force this day, and divide it equally among the inhabitants. Give every man above twenty years old an equal portion. Let all take share and share alike, and begin the world over again. Do this, and see where you would be at the end of fifty years. You would just have come round to the point where you began. You would just find things as unequal as before. Some would have worked, and some would have been idle. Some would have been always careless, and some always scheming. Some would have sold, and others would have bought. Some would have wasted, and others would have saved. And the end would be that some would be rich and others poor.

Practical Religion, 298.

One thing, however, we must never forget—no legislation, however clever and well-meant, will ever make all men rich and leave nobody poor. As long as the world stands, and human nature is unchanged, there will always be a vast amount of inequality. The Bible says, 'The poor shall never cease out of the land' (Deut. 15:11).

Charges and Addresses, 338.

ESCHATOLOGY

There is a time coming when sin shall be cast out from this world.—Wickedness shall not always flourish unpunished—Satan shall not always reign—creation shall not always groan, being burdened. There shall be a time of restitution of all things. There shall be a new heaven and a new earth, wherein dwelleth righteousness, and the earth shall be full of the knowledge of the Lord as the waters cover the sea (Rom. 8:22; Acts 3:21; 2 Pet. 3:13; Isa. 11:9).

Holiness, 418.

Let us dismiss from our minds the vain idea that nations will ever give up wars entirely, before Jesus Christ comes again. So long as the devil is the prince of this world, and the hearts of the many are unconverted, so long there must be strife and fighting. There will be no universal peace before the second advent of the Prince of peace. Then, and then only, men shall 'learn war no more' (Isa. 2:4). Let us cease to expect that missionaries and ministers will ever convert the world, and teach all mankind to love one another. They will do nothing of the kind. They were never intended to do it. They will call out a witnessing people who shall serve Christ in every land, but they will do no more. The bulk of mankind will always refuse to obey the gospel. The nations will always go on quarrelling, wrangling, and fighting. The last days of the earth shall be its worst days. The last war shall be the most fearful and terrible war that ever desolated the earth.

Expository Thoughts on Luke, 2.270.

The 'times of the Gentiles' I regard as the period between the first and second advents of Christ, during which the Gentile nations have a day of visitation and enjoy the privileges of the gospel.—These times will come to an end at last, as the old Jewish dispensation did, because of the hardness and unbelief of the Gentile churches. They too, because they continue not in God's goodness, will be cut off.—And when their time of visitation comes to an end, and they have been found as faithless and hardened as the Jews, then at last will the Jews be converted, and Jerusalem restored to its rightful possessors.

Expository Thoughts on Luke, 2.279.

Yet a little time, and faith shall be changed to sight, and hope to certainty: you shall see even as you have been seen, and know even as you have been known.

Old Paths, 112.

The longsuffering of God will at last have an end. The throne of grace will at length be taken down, and the throne of judgment will be set up in its place. The fountain of living waters shall at length be closed. The strait gate shall at last be barred and bolted. The day of grace will be passed and over. The day of reckoning with a sin laden world shall at length begin.

Practical Religion, 33-34.

ETERNAL SECURITY

Not one bone of his mystical body shall ever be broken. Not one lamb of his flock shall ever be left behind in the wilderness. He will raise to glory, in the last day, the whole flock entrusted to his charge, and not one shall be found missing.

Expository Thoughts on John, 1.260.

True believers may err and fail in many things, but they shall never finally be cast away. The will of God the Father, and the power of Christ the Son are both engaged on their side.

Expository Thoughts on John, 1.264.

Let all the world know that the Lord Jesus will not cast away his believing people because of shortcomings and infirmities. The husband does not put away his wife because he finds failings in her. The mother does not forsake her infant because it is weak, feeble and ignorant. And the Lord Christ does not cast off poor sinners who have committed their souls into his hands because he sees in them blemishes and imperfections.

Holiness, 281.

You might as well think to puck the stars out of heaven, as to puck one saint, however feeble, out of Christ's hand.

Practical Religion, 359.

ETHICS

How happy the world would be, if Christ's precepts were strictly obeyed! The chief causes of half the sorrows of mankind, are selfishness, strife, unkindness, and want of charity. Never was there a greater mistake than to suppose that vital Christianity interferes with human happiness. It is not having too much religion, but too little, that makes people gloomy, wretched, and miserable. Wherever Christ is best known and obeyed, there will always be found most real joy and peace.

Expository Thoughts on Luke, 1.143.

Any well-read man knows that the moral difference between the condition of the world before Christianity was planted, and since Christianity took root, is the difference between night and day, the kingdom of heaven and the kingdom of the devil.

Charges and Addresses, 236.

EVANGELICALISM

The first leading feature in Evangelical religion is *the absolute supremacy it assigns to Holy Scripture*, as the only rule of faith and practice, the only test of truth, the only judge of controversy.

Knots Untied, 4.

We hold that nothing whatever is needed between the soul of man the sinner and Christ the Saviour, but simple, childlike faith, and that all means, helps, ministers, and ordinances are useful just so far as they help this faith, but no further;—but that rested in and relied on as ends and not as means, they become downright poison to the soul.

Knots Untied, 6.

We maintain that the things which need most to be pressed on men's attention are those mighty works of the Holy Spirit: inward repentance, inward faith, inward hope, inward hatred of sin, and inward love to God's law. And we say that to tell men to take comfort in their baptism or church-membership, when these all-important graces are unknown, is not merely a mistake, but positive cruelty.

Knots Untied, 7.

We steadily refuse to exalt the Church above Christ, or to teach our people that membership of the Church is identical with membership of Christ. We refuse to assign it an authority for which we find no warrant either in Scripture or the Articles. We protest against the modern practice of first personifying the Church, then deifying it, and finally idolizing it. We hold that Church councils, Church synods, and Church convocations, may err, and that 'things ordained by them as necessary to salvation have neither strength nor authority, unless it may be declared that they be taken out of Holy Scripture.'

Knots Untied, 11.

EVANGELISM

We must go to work wisely. We must study the best avenues to their hearts, and the most likely ways of arresting their attention. There is a handle to every mind, and our chief aim must be to get hold of it.

Expository Thoughts on John, 1.142.

The time is short: the sand is running out of the glass of this old world; then redeem the time, and endeavour not to go to heaven alone.

Holiness, 411.

Where is our charity if we can see others going down to hell, and yet say nothing to them about Christ and salvation?—We may well doubt our own love to Christ if our hearts are never moved to speak of him.

Expository Thoughts on John, 1.163.

We must deal with many an unconverted man, as one half-asleep, half out of his mind, and not fully conscious of the state he is in. We must press the gospel on his notice again and again.

Expository Thoughts on Luke, 2.122.

Labour hard for the prosperity of the souls of others. Strive to bring a few more with you to heaven, and by all means to save some. Do something, by God's help, to make heaven more full and hell more empty.

Old Paths, 59.

You do not count him an enemy who gives you a bitter medicine to save your life. You do not count him an enemy who shakes you roughly from your sleep when your house is on fire. Surely you will not count me an enemy because I tell you strong truths for the benefit of your soul.

Old Paths, 83.

Think what a blessing to be allowed to speak one converting word!

Practical Religion, 43.

You cannot convert men, and give them eyes to see or hearts to feel. The Holy Ghost alone can do that. But you can be witnesses.

Charges and Addresses, 227.

EVIL

God does not love to make his creatures suffer. But God sees there are lessons which mankind could not learn unless evil was permitted: therefore, God permits it. The suffering of some tends to the good of many.

Expository Thoughts on John, 2.176
(also *Power and Sympathy of Christ,* 22-23).

FACTS

Facts speak louder than assertions. Facts are stubborn things.

Practical Religion, 258.

FAITH

Faith is the only hand that can carry the living water to our lips.

Holiness, 358.

Believing on Christ is coming to him, and coming to Christ is believing on him. It is that act of the soul which takes place when a man, feeling his own sins, and despairing of all other hope, commits himself to Christ for salvation, ventures on him, trusts him, and casts himself wholly on him. When a man turns to Christ empty that he may be filled—sick that he may be healed—hungry that he may be satisfied—thirsty that he may be refreshed—needy that he may be enriched—dying that he may have life—lost that he may be saved—guilty that he may be pardoned—sin-defiled that he may be cleansed—confessing that Christ alone can supply his need—then he comes to Christ.

Christmas Thoughts, 12-13.

There are no works to be done, no conditions to be fulfilled, no price to be paid, no wearing years of probation to be passed, before a sinner can be accepted with God. Let him only believe on Christ, and he is at once forgiven.

Expository Thoughts on John, 1.122.

We may feel ourselves poor, weak sinners. But do we believe?—We may fail and come short in many things. But do we believe?—He that has learned to feel his sins, and to trust Christ as a Saviour, has learned the two hardest and greatest lessons in Christianity. He has been in the best of schools. He has been taught by the Holy Ghost.

Expository Thoughts on John, 1.252.

You must learn to believe promises better than possessions; things unseen better than things seen; things in heaven out of sight better than things on earth before your eyes; the praise of the invisible God better than the praise of visible man.

Holiness, 195.

Faith is the root of a real Christian's character. Let your root be right, and your fruit will soon abound.

Holiness, 199.

Rest not on your own faith, but on Christ.

Holiness, 435.

To receive Christ is to accept him with a willing heart, and to take him as our Saviour.

Expository Thoughts on John, 1.15.

Faith is the root of saving religion. 'He that cometh unto God must believe that he is, and that he is a rewarder of them that diligently seek him' (Heb. 11:6). It is the hand by which the soul lays hold on Jesus Christ, and is united to him and saved. It is the secret of all Christian comfort, and spiritual prosperity. According to a man's faith will be his peace, his hope, his strength, his courage, his decision, and his victory over the world.

Expository Thoughts on Luke, 2.169.

Ignorance and unbelief may see nothing in the sufferings of Calvary but the cruel martyrdom of an innocent person. Faith will look far deeper. Faith will see in the death of Jesus the payment of man's enormous debt to God, and the complete salvation of all who believe.

Expository Thoughts on Luke, 2.384-85.

To attain and keep up the habit of looking steadily at invisible things, as if they were visible,—to set before our minds every day as grand realities, our souls, God, Christ, heaven, hell, judgment, eternity,—to cherish an abiding conviction that what we do not see is just as real as what we do see, and ten thousand times more important,—this, this is one way to be conquerors over the world.

Practical Religion, 286.

No inheritance of glory without sonship to God! No sonship to God without an interest in Christ! No interest in Christ without your own personal faith!

Practical Religion, 385.

Faith is the only hand that can carry the living water to our lips.

Upper Room, 98.

Faith is the first step towards heaven.

Upper Room, 126.

Faith and Holiness

I see many walking in darkness and having no light, from confused notions as to what faith is. They hear that saving faith will work by love and produce holiness, and not finding all this at once in themselves, they think they have no faith at all. They forget that these things are the fruits of faith, and not faith itself, and that to doubt whether we have faith, because we do not see them at once, is like doubting whether a tree is alive, because it does not bear fruit the very day we plant it in the ground.

Old Paths, 177.

Faith and Obedience

True believing will always be accompanied by godly living.

Expository Thoughts on John, 1.103.

Christians sometimes talk ignorantly about faith and works, as if they were things that could be compared with one another as equals, or opposed to one another as enemies.

Expository Thoughts on John, 1.254.

Small Beginnings

We must not set down a man as having no grace, because his first steps towards God are timid and wavering, and the first movements of his soul are uncertain, hesitating, and stamped with much imperfection.

Expository Thoughts on John, 1.85.

Have I not a right to say, 'The youngest faith will save a man's soul, if it only be true?' Behold the proof of it. This man's faith was only one day old; but it led him to Christ, and preserved him from hell.

Holiness, 245 (referring to the thief on the cross).

You say your faith is so small. But where is it said that none shall be saved except their faith be great?

Practical Religion, 438.

Weak Faith

The weakest faith is enough to join the soul to Christ, and to secure salvation. A trembling hand may receive a healing medicine. The feeblest infant may be heir to the richest possessions. The least faith gives a sinner a title to heaven as surely as the strongest.

Old Paths, 376.

FEAR OF MAN

What is the best remedy against the fear of man? How are we to overcome this powerful feeling, and break the chains which it throws around us? There is no remedy like that which our Lord recommends. We must supplant the fear of man by a higher and more powerful principle,—the fear of God. We must look away from those who can only hurt the body to him who has all dominion over the soul. We must turn our eyes from those who can only injure us in the life that now is, to him who can condemn us to eternal misery in the life to come. Armed with this mighty principle, we shall not play the coward.

Expository Thoughts on Luke, 2.45.

Herod was afraid of what his guests would think of him: so he did that which made him 'exceeding sorry',—he beheaded John the Baptist. Pilate feared offending the Jews: so he did that which he knew in his conscience was unjust,—he delivered up Jesus to be crucified. If this be not slavery, what is?

Thoughts for Young Men, 34.

Never be afraid of doing what is right.

Thoughts for Young Men, 35.

We are incessantly tempted to give way about little things, and to make compromises and concessions. We naturally dislike giving offence to others, and having frictions and collisions with relatives, friends, and neighbours. We do not like to be laughed at and ridiculed by the majority, and to feel that we are always in a minority in every company into which we go. I fear that too many are laughed out of heaven and laughed into hell.

Upper Room, 185-86.

FEELINGS

A man may have many religious feelings about Christ, without any saving religion.

Expository Thoughts on John, 2.64.

Thousands have no more religious feeling than a cat or dog. But oh, beware lest you make a Christ of your feelings and sensations! They are poor, uncertain things and sadly dependent on our bodies and outward circumstances. Rest only on Christ.

Holiness, 436.

FORGIVENESS

He is far more willing to forgive than men are to be forgiven, and far more ready to pardon than men are to be pardoned. There is in his almighty heart an infinite willingness to put away man's transgressions.

Expository Thoughts on Luke, 2.379.

FORMALISM

Whether they hear law or gospel, truth or error, it is all the same to them. They remember nothing afterwards. They take off their form of religion with their Sunday clothes, and return to the world.

Practical Religion, 30.

None seem to become so desperately hard as those who are continually repeating holy words and handling holy things, while their hearts are running after sin and the world.

Practical Religion, 250.

A painted fire cannot warm, and a painted banquet cannot satisfy hunger, and a formal religion cannot bring peace to the soul.

Practical Religion, 250.

He who said to the man without the wedding garment, 'Friend, how camest thou in hither?' will not be deceived by a little cloak of outward religion.

Practical Religion, 251.

FRIENDSHIPS

Remember the words of Solomon: 'He that walketh with wise men shall be wise; but a companion of fools shall be destroyed' (Prov. 13:20). But depend on it, bad company in the life that now is, is the sure way to procure worse company in the life to come.

Thoughts for Young Men, 53.

GENEROSITY

Where are the Samaritans, we may well ask, in this land of Bibles and Testaments?

Upper Room, 86.

GIFTS

Men forget that gifts without grace save no one's soul, and are the characteristic of Satan himself. Grace, on the contrary, is an everlasting inheritance, and, lowly and despised as its possessor may be, will land him safe in glory. He that has gifts without grace is dead in sins, however splendid his gifts may be. But he that has grace without gifts is alive to God, however unlearned and ignorant he may appear to man. And 'a living dog is better than a dead lion' (Eccles. 9:4).

Expository Thoughts on Luke, 1.274-75.

GOD

The grand secret of knowing God is to draw near to him through Jesus Christ.

Expository Thoughts on John, 2.57.

Hatred of God

Unconverted men would kill God, if they could get at him.

Expository Thoughts on Matthew, 311 (paraphrase of Jonathan Edwards).

Ignorance of God

Ignorance of Christ is the root of ignorance of God. Wrong at the starting point, the whole sum of a man's religion is full of error.

Expository Thoughts on John, 2.57.

Love of God

To say that God loves us because Christ died for us, is wretched theology indeed. But to say that Christ came into the world in consequence of the love of God, is scriptural truth.

Expository Thoughts on John, 1.112.

It is not true that all mankind will be finally saved. But let us not fly into the extreme of denying God's universal compassion. It is true that God 'loves the world.'—Let us maintain jealously the privileges of God's elect. It is true that they are loved with a special love, and will be loved to all eternity. But let us not exclude any man or woman from the pale of God's kindness and compassion. We have no right to pare down the meaning of words when Jesus says, 'God loved the world'. The heart of God is far wider than that of man. There is a sense in which the Father loves all mankind.

Old Paths, 357.

Omniscience of God

Do nothing you would not like God to see. *Say* nothing you would not like God to hear. *Write* nothing you would not like God to read. *Go* to no place where you would not like God to find you. *Read* no book of which you would not like God to say, 'Show it me.' Never spend your time in such a way that you would not like to have God say, 'What art thou doing?'

Thoughts for Young Men, 62.

Power of God

In truth, with God it is just as easy to do a thing as to say it. Whatever he promises, he is certain to perform.

Holiness, 362 (also *Upper Room,* 102).

Sovereignty of God

Of all the doctrines of the Bible none is so offensive to human nature as the doctrine of God's sovereignty. To be told that God is great, and just, and holy, and pure, man can bear. But to be told that 'he hath mercy on whom he will have mercy,'—that he 'giveth no account of his matters,'—that it is 'not of him that willeth, nor of him that runneth, but of God that showeth mercy,'—these are truths that natural man cannot stand. They often call forth all his enmity against God, and fill him with wrath. Nothing, in short, will make him submit to them but the humbling teaching of the Holy Ghost.

Expository Thoughts on Luke, 1.94.

GOOD WORKS

If God so loved us as to give his Son for our souls, we should count it a privilege and not a burden, to give what we can to do good to men.

Old Paths, 362.

The plain truth is that many believers in the present day seem so dreadfully afraid of doing harm that they hardly ever dare to do good.

Practical Religion, 194.

GOSPEL

This is the glory and excellence of the gospel. It meets man as he really is. It takes him as it finds him. It goes down to the level to which sin has brought him, and offers to raise him up. It tells him of a remedy equal to his disease,—a great remedy for a great disease,—a great forgiveness for great sinners.

Old Paths, 173.

The story of the crucified Lamb of God has proved, in every age, the power of God unto salvation.

Expository Thoughts on John, 1.49.

Let us never doubt for a moment, that the preaching of Christ crucified—the old story of his blood, and righteousness, and substitution,—is enough for all the spiritual necessities of all mankind.

Expository Thoughts on John, 1.229.

Hospitals discharge many cases as incurable. But there are no incurable cases under the gospel. Any sinner may be healed, if he will only come to Christ.

Expository Thoughts on Luke, 2.217.

This is the only lever which has ever turned the world upside down hitherto, and made men forsake their sins. And if this will not, nothing will.

Old Paths, 240-41.

We must learn to distinguish between things that are of the essence of the gospel and things which are of the perfection of the gospel.

Christian Leaders of the Eighteenth Century, 71.

We want the story of Christ dying for our sins, and rising again for our justification. We want Christ the mediator, Christ the substitute, Christ the intercessor, Christ the redeemer, in order to meet with confidence the king of terrors, and to say, 'Oh death, where is they sting? Oh grave, where is thy victory?'

Charges and Addresses, 65.

Apply this little simple parable to the gospel. Regard it as a medicine sent down from heaven, for the curing of man's spiritual disease, by a Physician of infinite skill and power; a medicine of singular efficacy, which man with all his wisdom could never have devised.

Knots Untied, 19.

Free Offer of the Gospel

We must hold firmly that pardon and peace are to be offered freely through Christ to every man and woman without exception. We never know who they are that God will draw, and have nothing to do with it. Our duty is to invite all, and leave it to God to choose the vessels of mercy.

Expository Thoughts on John, 1.272.

The door of hope which the gospel reveals to sinners is very wide open. Let us leave it open as we find it. Let us not attempt, in narrow-minded ignorance, to shut it. We should never be afraid to maintain that Christ is 'able to save to the uttermost,' and that the vilest of sinners may be freely forgiven if they will only come to him. We should offer the gospel boldly to the worst and wickedest.

Expository Thoughts on Luke, 2.216-17.

Seek durable riches—a treasure that cannot be taken from you—a city which hath lasting foundations. Do as the Apostle Paul did. Give yourself to the Lord Jesus Christ, and seek that incorruptible crown he is ready to bestow. Take his yoke upon you, and learn of him. Come away from a world which will never really satisfy you, and from sin which will bite like a serpent, if you cleave to it, at last. Come to the Lord Jesus as lowly sinners, and he will receive you, pardon you, give you his renewing Spirit, fill you with peace. This shall give you more real comfort than the world has ever done. There is a gulf in your heart which nothing but the peace of Christ can fill. Enter in and share our privileges. Come with us, and sit down by our side.

Holiness, 165.

The Lord Jesus invites you. It is enough that you feel thirsting, and desire to be saved. *Come*: come to Christ without delay. Who ever came to the fountain for sin and found it dry? Who ever went unsatisfied away?

Holiness, 369.

Escape for your life: flee from the wrath to come. Time is short: eternity is near. Life is uncertain: judgment is sure. Arise and call upon God. The throne of grace is yet standing: the Lord Jesus Christ is yet waiting to be gracious. The promises of the gospel are wide, broad, full, and free: lay hold upon them this day. Repent, and believe the gospel: repent, and be converted.

Old Paths, 317.

The doctrine of election was never meant to prevent *the fullest, freest offer of salvation* to every sinner. In preaching and trying to do good we are warranted and commanded to set an open door before every man, woman, and child, and to invite everyone to come in.

We know not who are God's elect, and whom he means to call and convert. Our duty is to invite all.

Old Paths, 439.

Mark well, that the Lord Jesus does not bid the labouring and heavy laden 'go and work.' Those words would carry no comfort to heavy consciences. It would be like requiring labour from an exhausted man. No! He bids them 'Come.' He does not say, 'Pay me what thou owest.' That demand would drive a broken heart into despair. It would be like claiming a debt from a ruined bankrupt. No! He says, 'Come!' He does not say, 'Stand still and wait.' That command would only be a mockery. It would be like promising to give medicine at the end of a week to one at the point of death. No! He says, 'Come!' Today—at once—without any delay, 'Come unto me.'

Christmas Thoughts, 11.

Dismiss from your mind for ever all idea of worthiness, merit, and fitness in yourself. Throw away notions of goodness, righteousness, and deserts. Think not that you can bring anything to recommend you, or to make you deserving of Christ's notice. You must come to him as a poor, guilty, undeserving sinner, or you might just as well not come at all. 'To him that worketh not but believeth on him that justifieth the ungodly, his faith is counted for righteousness' (Rom. 4:5). It is the peculiar mark of the faith that justifies and saves, that it brings to Christ nothing but an empty hand.

Christmas Thoughts, 14.

GRACE

Believers become what they are solely and entirely by the grace of God.

Expository Thoughts on John, 1.16.

We should consider nothing impossible, and regard no sinner as beyond the reach of the grace of God.

Expository Thoughts on John, 1.160.

Let the religion which we aim to possess be a religion in which grace is the main thing. Let it not content us to be able to speak eloquently, or preach powerfully, or reason ably, or argue cleverly, or profess loudly, or talk fluently. Let it not satisfy us to know the whole system of Christian doctrines, and to have texts and words at our command. These things are all well in their way. They are not to be undervalued. They have their use. But these things are not the grace of God, and they will not deliver us from hell.

Expository Thoughts on Luke, 1.275.

Grace is the fountain of life from which our salvation flows. Grace is the agency through which our spiritual life is kept up.

Knots Untied, 395.

Beginnings of Grace

We must not set down a man as having no grace, because his first steps towards God are timid and wavering, and the first movements of his soul are uncertain, hesitating, and stamped with much imperfection. We must remember our Lord's reception of Nicodemus.

Expository Thoughts on John, 1.85.

Growth in Grace

The Christian who has ceased to say, 'I must see, and then I will believe,' and has learned to say, 'I believe, and by and by I shall see,' has reached a high degree in the school of Christ.

Expository Thoughts on John, 2.204
(also *Power and Sympathy of Christ,* 84).

When I speak of a man 'growing in grace,' I mean simply this—that his sense of sin is becoming deeper, his faith stronger, his hope brighter, his love more extensive, his spiritual-mindedness more marked. He feels more of the power of godliness in his own heart. He manifests more of it in his life. He is going on from strength to strength, from faith to faith, and from grace to grace.

Holiness, 115-16.

Grace is sometimes so weak and feeble, that it looks like nature. Nature is sometimes so plausible and well dressed, that it looks like grace.

Practical Religion, 419.

Sovereign Grace

Claim upon God we have none. Right to expect anything from God we have none. Worthiness to deserve anything from God we have none. All that we have we have received. All that we are we owe to God's sovereign, distinguishing grace.

Expository Thoughts on Luke, 2.170.

GREATNESS

The measure of greatness which is common among men is utterly false and deceptive. Princes and potentates, conquerors and leaders of armies, statesmen and philosophers, artists and authors,—these are the kind of men whom the world calls 'great.' Such greatness is not recognized among the angels of God.

Expository Thoughts on Luke, 1.10-11.

GRIMSHAW, WILLIAM

None ever worked harder than he did in his calling, and few worked so hard. He seldom preached less than twenty, and often nearly thirty times in a week.

Christian Leaders of the Eighteenth Century, 102.

'When I die I shall then have my greatest grief and my greatest joy,—my greatest grief that I have done so little for Jesus, and my greatest joy that Jesus has done so much for me. My last words shall be, *Here goes an unprofitable servant!*'

Christian Leaders of the Eighteenth Century, 103.

GUILT

The measure of men's guilt is the quantity of light they enjoy.

Charges and Addresses, 202.

HAPPINESS

Riches, and rank, and place, and power, and learning, and amusements, are utterly unable to fill the soul. He that only drinks of these waters is sure to thirst again. Every Ahab finds a Naboth's vineyard hard by his palace, and every Haman sees a Mordecai at the gate. There is no heart-satisfaction in this world, until we believe on Christ. Jesus alone can fill up the empty places of our inward man. Jesus alone can give solid, lasting, enduring happiness.

Expository Thoughts on John, 1.143.

So long as you do not quarrel with sin, you will never be a truly happy man.

Old Paths, 390.

True happiness is *not perfect freedom from sorrow and discomfort.* Let that never be forgotten. If it were so, there would be no such thing as happiness in the world. Such happiness is for angels who have never fallen, and not for man.

Practical Religion, 219.

It is an utter mistake to suppose that *pleasure seeking and amusements alone* can give happiness. Of all roads that men can take in order to be happy, this is the one that is most completely wrong.

Practical Religion, 225.

There are degrees of grace and degrees of faith. Those who have most faith and grace will have most happiness.

Practical Religion, 234.

The plain truth is that without Christ there is no happiness in this world. He alone can give the Comforter who abideth for ever. He is the sun; without him men never feel warm. He is the light; without him men are always in the dark. He is the bread; without him men are always starving. He is the living water; without him men are always athirst. Give them what you like,—place them where you please,—surround them with all the comforts you can imagine,—it makes no difference. Separate from Christ, the Prince of Peace, a man cannot be happy.

Practical Religion, 236.

Go on, if you will, imagining that true happiness is to be found in the good things of this world. Seek it, if you will, in revelling and banqueting, in dancing and merry-making, in races and theatres, in field-sports and cards. Seek it, if you will, in reading and scientific pursuits, in music and painting, in politics and business. Seek it, but you will never overtake it, unless you change your plan. Real heart-rest is never to be found except in heart-union with Jesus Christ.

Christmas Thoughts, 23-24.

HEART

The heart is the man. It is the seat of all spiritual life, and health, and strength, and growth. It is the hinge and turning-point in the condition of man's soul.

Old Paths, 320.

Our hearts are like the earth on which we tread; let it alone, and it is sure to bear weeds.

Upper Room, 245.

You may be clear, correct, and sound in your religious opinions. But all this time you may be walking in the broad way which leadeth to destruction. It is your heart which is the main point.

Old Paths, 319.

HEAVEN

Sanctification … is *absolutely necessary in order to train and prepare us for heaven.* Most men hope to go to heaven when they die; but few, it may be feared, take the trouble to consider whether they would enjoy heaven if they got there.

Holiness, 31.

One cheering word is this,—'I go to prepare a place for you.' Heaven is a prepared place for a prepared people: a place which we shall find Christ himself has made ready for true Christians. He has prepared it by procuring a right for every sinner who believes to enter in. None can stop us, and say we have no business there.—He has prepared it by going before us as our Head and Representative, and taking possession of it for all the members of his mystical body. As our Forerunner he has marched in, leading captivity captive, and has planted his banner in the land of glory.—He has prepared it by carrying our names with him as our High Priest into the holy of holies, and making angels ready to receive us. They that enter heaven will find they are neither unknown nor unexpected.

Expository Thoughts on John, 3.39.

We shall drink out of the river of his pleasures and thirst no more.

Holiness, 370.

The man who hopes to dwell in heaven, should have some experimental acquaintance with the language of its inhabitants.

Expository Thoughts on Luke, 1.46.

A few more tossings to and fro on the waves of this troublesome world,—a few more battles and conflicts with our spiritual enemy,—a few more years of tears and partings, of working and suffering, of crosses and cares, of disappointments and vexations,—and then, then we shall be at home. The harbour lights are already in view: the haven of rest is not far off. *There* we shall find all that we have hoped for, and find that it was a million times better than our hopes. *There* we shall find all the saints,—and no sin, no cares of this world, no money, no sickness, no death, no devil. *There*, above all, we shall find Jesus, and be ever with the Lord! (1 Thess. 4:17).

Old Paths, 112-13.

There are many things which are not needful. Riches are not needful. Health is not needful. Fine clothes are not needful. Noble friends are not needful. The favour of the world is not needful. Gifts and learning are not needful. Millions have reached heaven without these things. Thousands are reaching heaven every year without them. But no one ever reached heaven without 'repentance toward God, and faith toward our Lord Jesus Christ.'

Old Paths, 389.

We shall no longer lament with Jonah over withered gourds.

Practical Religion, 396.

Heaven is a prepared place for a prepared people.

Practical Religion, 410.

There is a good time coming for all who have come to Christ and committed their souls into his keeping. They shall remember all the way by which they have been led, and see the wisdom of every step in the way. They shall wonder that they ever doubted the kindness and love of their Shepherd.

Christmas Thoughts, 28.

Some of God's family are safe *in heaven.* They are at rest in that place which the Lord Jesus expressly calls 'Paradise' (Luke 23:43). They have finished their course. They have fought their battle. They have done their appointed work. They have learned their lessons. They have carried their cross. They have passed through the waves of this troublesome world and reached the harbour. Little as we know about them we know that they are happy. They are no longer troubled by sin and temptation. They have said goodbye for ever to poverty and anxiety, to pain and sickness, to sorrow and tears. They are with Christ himself, who loved them and gave himself for them, and in his company they must needs be happy (Phil. 1:23).

Christmas Thoughts, 61-62.

You see only a small body of believers in this present time. But you must not forget that a great company has got safe to heaven already, and that when all are assembled at the last day they will be 'a multitude which no man can number' (Rev. 7:9). You only see that part of the family which is struggling on earth. You must never forget that the greater part of the family has got home and is resting in heaven. You see the militant part but not the triumphant. You see the part that is carrying the cross, but not the part which is safe in Paradise. The family of God is far more rich and glorious than you suppose.

Christmas Thoughts, 65-66.

There is a Judas Iscariot at every communion table, and a Demas in every apostolic company; and wherever the sons of God come together, Satan is sure to appear among them. But all this shall come to an end one day. Our Lord shall at length present to the Father a perfect church, having neither spot nor wrinkle, nor any such thing.

Christmas Thoughts, 108-9.

Without election, intercession, and regeneration, there is not one soul who would get to heaven.

Upper Room, 234-35.

HELL

I hold it to be impossible to deal honestly with the Bible, and to avoid the conclusions to which it will lead us on this point. If words mean anything, there is such a place as hell. If texts are to be interpreted fairly, there are those who will be cast into it. If language has any sense belonging to it, hell is for ever.

Holiness, 234.

Give me the preaching which keeps back nothing that God has revealed. You may call it stern and harsh; you may tell us that to frighten people is not the way to do them good. But you are forgetting that the grand object of the gospel is to persuade men to 'flee from the wrath to come,' and that it is vain to expect men to flee unless they are afraid.

Holiness, 238.

There is a hell after death. The state of the wicked man after this life is not annihilation. There is a hell which ought to be feared. There is a just God who will finally cast into hell the obstinately impenitent and unbelieving.

Expository Thoughts on Luke, 2.47.

There is but a step between the unbeliever and the worm that never dies, and the fire that is not quenched. He is literally hanging over the brink of the bottomless pit. Sudden death to the saint is sudden glory; but sudden death to the unconverted sinner is sudden hell.

Old Paths, 481.

Men are apt to forget that it does not require great open sins to be sinned in order to ruin a soul for ever. They have only to go on hearing without believing, listening without repenting, going to church without going to Christ, and by and by they will find themselves in hell!

Expository Thoughts on Matthew, 78.

If hell has an end, heaven has an end too. They both stand or fall together.

Practical Religion, 433.

There are two ways of coming down from the top of a church steeple; one is to jump down,—and the other is to come down by the steps: but both will lead you to the bottom. So also there are two ways of going to hell; one is to walk into it with your eyes open,—few people do that; the other is to go down by the steps of little sins,—and that way, I fear, is only too common.

Thoughts for Young Men, 57.

HOLINESS

Sound Protestant and Evangelical doctrine is useless if it is not accompanied by a holy life.

Holiness, xii.

The real cause of many people's dislike to the gospel, is the holiness of living which it demands.

Expository Thoughts on John, 2.3.

The only way to make men holy, is to teach and preach free and full forgiveness through Jesus Christ. The secret of being holy ourselves, is to know and feel that Christ has pardoned our sins. Peace with God is the only root that will bear the fruit of holiness. Forgiveness must go before sanctification. We shall do nothing till we are reconciled to God.—This is the first step in religion. We must work from life, and not for life. Our best works before we are justified are little better than splendid sins.—We must live by faith in the Son of God, and then, and not till then, we shall walk in his ways. The heart which has experienced the pardoning love of Christ, is the heart which loves Christ, and strives to glorify him.

Expository Thoughts on Luke, 1.182.

Sanctification, again, is *a thing which depends greatly on a diligent use of scriptural means.* When I speak of 'means', I have in view Bible-reading, private prayer, regular attendance on public worship, regular hearing of God's Word, and regular reception of the Lord's supper. I lay it down as a simple matter of fact, that no one who is careless about such things must ever expect to make much progress in sanctification. I can find no record of any eminent saint who ever neglected them.

Holiness, 28.

People who are habitually giving way to peevish and cross tempers in daily life, and are constantly sharp with their tongues, and disagreeable to all around them—spiteful people, vindictive people, revengeful people, malicious people—of whom, alas, the world is only too full!—all such know little, as they should know, about sanctification.

Holiness, 39.

Faith that does not purify the heart and life, is not faith at all. Grace that cannot be seen, like light, and tasted, like salt, is not grace, but hypocrisy. The man who professes to know Christ and trust him, while he cleaves to sin and the world, is going down to hell with a lie in his right hand. The heart that has really tasted the grace of Christ, will instinctively hate sin.

Expository Thoughts on Luke, 2.219.

The great apostle, who said 'I fight,—I labour,—I keep under my body and bring it into subjection' (1 Cor. 9:27), would have been amazed to hear of *sanctification without personal exertion*, and to be told that believers only need to sit still, and everything will be done for them!

Practical Religion, 11.

The purity that God desires to see is not the purity of bodily washing and fasting, of holy water and self-imposed asceticism, but purity of heart.

Expository Thoughts on John, 2.215
(also *Power and Sympathy of Christ,* 108).

With all this immense growth of external Christianity, is there any corresponding growth of vital godliness? Is there more faith, repentance, and holiness among the worshippers in our churches? Is there more of that saving faith without which it is impossible to please God, more of that repentance unto salvation without which a man must perish, and more of that holiness without which no man shall see the Lord? Is our Lord Jesus Christ more known and trusted and loved and obeyed?

Charges and Addresses, 103.

Holiness, How?

I have little doubt that many look on eminent holiness as a kind of special gift, which none but a few must pretend to aim at. They admire it at a distance, in books: they think it beautiful when they see an example near themselves. But as to its being a thing within the reach of any but a very few, such a notion never seems to enter their minds. In short, they consider it a kind of monopoly granted to a few favoured believers, but certainly not to all.

Now I believe that this is a most dangerous mistake. I believe that spiritual, as well as natural, greatness depends far more on the use of means within everybody's reach, than on anything else.

Practical Religion, 71.

I believe you cannot look much at the cross without feeling your will sanctified, and your tastes made more spiritual. As the sun gazed upon makes everything else look dark and dim, so does the cross darken the false splendour of this world.

Old Paths, 245.

Holiness in Christ

Would you be holy? Would you become a new creature? Then you must *begin with Christ.* You will do just nothing at all, and make no progress till you feel your sin and weakness, and flee to him. He is the root and beginning of all holiness, and the way to be holy is to come to him by faith and be joined to him.

Holiness, 67.

I do not mean for a moment to undervalue the work of the Spirit. But this I say, that no man is ever holy till he comes to Christ and is united to him.

Holiness, 425.

I pity those who try to be holy without Christ! Your labour is all in vain. You are putting money in a bag with holes.

Holiness, 426.

Necessity of Holiness

The question will not be how we talked and what we professed, but how we lived and what we did. Let no man deceive himself on this point. If anything is certain about the future, it is certain that there will be a judgment; and if anything is certain about judgment, it is certain that men's 'works' and 'doings' will be considered and examined in it (John 5:29; 2 Cor. 5:10; Rev. 20:13).

Holiness, 31.

Are believers said to be elect?—it is 'through sanctification of the Spirit.' Are they predestinated?—it is 'to be conformed to the image of God's Son.' Are they chosen?—it is 'that they may be holy.' Are they called?—it is 'with a holy calling.' Are they afflicted?—it is that they may be 'partakers of holiness.' Jesus is a complete Saviour. He does not merely take away the guilt of a believer's sin, he does more—he breaks its power (1 Peter 1:2; Rom. 8:29; Eph. 1:4; Heb. 12:10.).

Holiness, 56.

HOLY SPIRIT

The Holy Ghost can incline even the richest of men to seek treasure in heaven. He can dispose even kings to cast their crowns at the feet of Jesus, and count all things but loss for the sake of the kingdom of God.

Expository Thoughts on Matthew, 195.

A bramble will never bear grapes, however much it may be cultivated, and a natural man will never be a godly man without the Spirit.

Expository Thoughts on John, 1.97.

There is no self-curative power in man. He will always go on reproducing himself. To become spiritual and fit for communion with God, nothing less is required than the entrance of the Spirit of God into our hearts.

Expository Thoughts on John, 1.97.

The way in which the Spirit leads all God's people is always one and the same. But the paths by which they are severally brought into that road are often widely different.

Expository Thoughts on John, 1.169.

The mighty agent by whom the Lord Jesus Christ carries out this work in the members of his church is without doubt the Holy Ghost. He it is who is ever renewing, awakening, convincing, leading to the cross, transforming, taking out of the world stone after stone, and adding to the mystical building.

Holiness, 291.

Without the Holy Ghost *no man ever turns to God, repents, believes, and obeys.*

Old Paths, 254.

When the Spirit really begins a work of conversion, he always carries that work to perfection. He effects miraculous changes. He turns the character upside down. He causes old things to pass away, and all things to become new. In a word, the Holy Ghost is Almighty. With him nothing is impossible.

Old Paths, 260-61.

Where the Holy Ghost is, there will always be *deep conviction of sin, and true repentance for it.* It is his special office to convince of sin (John 16:8).

Old Paths, 264.

Repentance toward God,—faith toward our Lord Jesus Christ,—holiness of heart and life,—habits of real private prayer,—love and reverence toward God's word,—these are the real proofs of the indwelling of the Holy Ghost in a man's soul.

Old Paths, 266.

The indwelling of God the Holy Spirit is the common mark of all true believers in Christ. It is the Shepherd's mark on the flock of the Lord Jesus, distinguishing them from the rest of the world.

Old Paths, 275.

Baptism of the Holy Spirit

There is a baptism which is absolutely necessary to salvation, beyond all question. There is a baptism without which no one, whether old or young, has over gone to heaven. But what baptism is this? It is not the baptism of *water*, but the inward baptism which the Holy Ghost gives to the *heart*. It is not a baptism which any man can offer, whether ordained or unordained.

Knots Untied, 101.

Fruits of the Spirit

I tell you plainly that you are deceiving yourself, if you dream that the Spirit is in a man, when his presence cannot be seen. Go and learn this day that the presence of the Holy Ghost is to be tested, not by the name in the register, or the place in the family pew, but by the visible fruits in a man's life.

Old Paths, 261-62.

I do not expect to behold the Holy Ghost with my bodily eyes, or to touch him with my hands. But I need no angel to come down to show me where he dwells; I need no vision from heaven to tell me where I may find him. Only show me a man in whom the fruits of the Spirit are to be seen, and I see one who 'has the Spirit'. I will not doubt the inward presence of the almighty *cause,* when I see the outward fact of an evident *effect.*

Old Paths, 282.

Holy Spirit and Effectual Calling

The Spirit of Christ calls them out from the world, and separates them as effectually as if a wall were built between them and it. He puts in them new hearts, new minds, new tastes, new desires, new sorrows, new joys, new wishes, new pleasures, new longings. He gives them new eyes, new ears, new affections, new opinions. He makes them new creatures; they are born again, and with a new birth they begin a new existence.

Upper Room, 234.

Holy Spirit and Illumination

Pride, and prejudice, and love of the world blind our intellects, and throw a veil over the eyes of our minds in the reading of the Scriptures. We see the words, but do not thoroughly understand them until we are taught from above.

Expository Thoughts on Luke, 2.383-84.

Holy Spirit and Salvation

A sense of sin, guilt, and poverty of soul, is the first stone laid by the Holy Ghost, when he builds a spiritual temple. He convinces of sin. Light was the first thing called into being in the material creation (Gen. 1:3). Light about our own state is the first work in the new creation. … It is not when we begin to feel good, but when we feel bad, that we take the first step towards heaven.

Upper Room, 95.

He who moved on the face of the waters before those wonderful words were spoken, 'Let there be light', is he who moves over sinners' souls, and takes their natural darkness away. Great indeed is the invisible power of the Holy Ghost! He can soften that which is hard. He can bend that which is stiff and stubborn. He can give eyes to the spiritually blind, ears to the spiritually deaf, tongues to the spiritually dumb, feet to the spiritually lame, warmth to the spiritually cold, knowledge to the spiritually ignorant, and life to the spiritually dead. 'None teacheth like him!' (Job 36:22).

Old Paths, 311.

The age of spiritual miracles is not yet past! Dead souls in our congregations can yet be raised; blind eyes can yet be made to see; dumb prayerless tongues can yet be taught to pray. No one ought ever to despair. When Christ has left heaven, and laid down his office as the Saviour of sinners,—when the Holy Ghost has ceased to dwell in hearts, and is no longer God,—then, and not till then, men and women may say, 'We cannot be converted'.

Old Paths, 312.

Holy Spirit and Sanctification

The Holy Ghost never works in a person's soul without producing *some* perceptible results in character and conduct.

Upper Room, 116.

Spiritual Warfare

The presence of the Holy Ghost may be known by inward warfare as well as by inward peace. He that has been taught to rest and hope in Christ, will always be one who fights and wars with sin.

Old Paths, 291.

HOPE

Let us learn never to despair about the cause of God's truth, however black and unfavourable its prospects may appear. At the very time when things seem hopeless, God may be preparing a mighty deliverance. At the very season when Satan's kingdom seems to be triumphing, the 'little stone, cut without hands,' may be on the point of crushing it to pieces. The darkest hour of the night is often that which just precedes the day.

Expository Thoughts on Luke, 1.65.

The dying thief in London, who was visited by a City Missionary, and found utterly ignorant of Christianity, laid hold on one single fact in a chapter of St Luke's Gospel which was read to him, and found comfort in it. That fact was the story of the penitent thief. 'Sir', he said, when visited the second time, 'are there any more thieves in that book from which you read yesterday?'

Old Paths, 93.

If there is light in a house it will shine through the windows: if there is any real hope in a man's soul it will be seen in his ways.

Old Paths, 100.

I allow that there are many believers who live far below their privileges, and seem to know nothing of joy and peace in believing. But did you ever ask any of these people whether they would give up the position in religion they have reached, and go back to the world? Did you ever ask them, after all their groanings, and doubtings, and fearings, whether they think they would be happier if they ceased to follow hard after Christ? *Did you ever ask those questions?* I am certain if you did, that the weakest and lowest believers would all give you one answer. I am certain they would tell you that they would rather cling to their little scrap of hope in Christ, than possess the world.

Practical Religion, 238.

HUMAN NATURE

Above all, the natural heart generally likes the praise of others, shrinks from collision, and loves to be thought charitable and liberal.

Holiness, 397.

Human nature is the same evil thing everywhere.

Practical Religion, 231.

The strongest proof of our common origin is to be found in the painful uniformity of man's moral nature, whatever be the colour of his skin. Go where you will on the globe, and observe what men and women are everywhere. Go to the heart of Africa or China, or to the remotest island of the Pacific Ocean, and mark the result of your investigations. I boldly assert that everywhere, and in every climate, you will find the moral nature of the human race exactly the same. Everywhere you will find men and women are naturally wicked, corrupt, selfish, proud, lazy, deceitful, godless,—servants of lusts and passions.

Upper Room, 77-78.

Tell them to do some great thing, to mortify their bodies, to go on pilgrimage, to give all their goods to feed the poor, and so to merit salvation, and they will try to do as they are bid. Tell them to throw overboard all idea of merit, working, or doing, and to come to Christ as empty sinners, with nothing in their hands, and, like Naaman, they are ready to turn away in disdain (2 Kings 5:12). Human nature is always the same in every age.

Upper Room, 98-99.

Leave man without a Bible, and he will have a religion of some kind, for human nature, corrupt as it is, must have a God. But it will be a religion without light, or peace, or hope.

Upper Room, 133.

HUMILITY

Humility is the first step toward heaven, and the true way to honour. 'He that humbleth himself shall be exalted' (Luke 18:14).

Expository Thoughts on John, 1.236.

The nearer we get to heaven, the more we are clothed with humility

Holiness, 11-12.

Superficial and shallow professors in the warmth of their first love may talk, if they will, of perfection. The great saints, in every era of Church history, from St Paul down to this day, have always been 'clothed with humility.'

Holiness, 377.

Humility is the highest grace that can adorn the Christian character. It is a true saying of an old divine, that 'a man has just so much Christianity as he has humility.' It is the grace, which of all is most becoming to human nature. Above all, it is the grace which is within the reach of every converted person. All are not rich. All are not learned. All are not highly gifted. All are not preachers. But all children of God may be clothed with humility.

Expository Thoughts on Luke, 1.28

The plain truth is, that we are all too ready to say, 'We are the men, and wisdom shall die with us' (Job 12:2). We forget that no church on earth has an absolute monopoly of all wisdom, and that people may be right in the main, without agreeing with us. We must learn to be thankful if sin is opposed, and the gospel preached, and the devil's kingdom pulled down, though the work may not be done exactly in the way we like. We must try to believe that men may be true-hearted followers of Jesus Christ, and yet for some wise reason may be kept back from seeing all things in religion just as we do. Above all, we must praise God if souls are converted, and Christ is magnified,—no matter who the preacher may be, and to what church he may belong.

Expository Thoughts on Luke, 1.251-52.

The root of humility is right *knowledge*. The man who really knows himself and his own heart,—who knows God and his infinite majesty and holiness,—who knows Christ, and the price at which he was redeemed,—that man will never be a proud man. He will count himself, like Jacob, unworthy of the least of all God's mercies. He will say of himself, like Job, 'I am vile.' He will cry, like Paul, 'I am chief of sinners' (Gen. 32:10; Job 40:4; 1 Tim. 1:15). He will think anything good enough for him. In lowliness of mind he will esteem every one else to be better than himself (Phil. 2:3). Ignorance—nothing but sheer ignorance—ignorance of self, of God, and of Christ, is the real secret of pride.

Expository Thoughts on Luke, 2.114-15.

We have nothing to boast of. All that we have we have received.

Expository Thoughts on Luke, 2.226.

I am satisfied to believe that all God's work is well done. It is enough for me to be in the King's court, without being of the King's counsel.

Old Paths, 285.

The wisest men would tell you they are always learners, and are humbled to find after all how little they know. The great Sir Isaac Newton used to say that he felt himself no better than a little child who had picked up a few precious stones on the shore of the sea of knowledge.

Thoughts for Young Men, 23.

HYMNS

Good hymns are an immense blessing to the church of Christ. I believe the last day alone will show the world the real amount of good they have done. They suit all, both rich and poor. There is an elevating, stirring, soothing, spiritualizing, effect about a thoroughly good hymn, which nothing else can produce. It sticks in men's memories when texts are forgotten. It trains men for heaven, where praise is one of the principal occupations. Preaching and praying shall one day cease for ever; but praise shall never die.

Christian Leaders of the Eighteenth Century, 360.

HYPOCRISY

There is always more hope of one who honestly and bluntly confesses sin, than of a smooth-tongued hypocrite.

Expository Thoughts on John, 1.153.

We may be sure that all is not gold that glitters, and that many a professor is rotten at heart. It was so even under our Lord's ministry and much more now.

Expository Thoughts on John, 1.247.

External devoutness of conduct, a grave face, and a bowed head, and a solemn countenance, and a loud amen, are all abominable in God's sight, so long as our hearts are not washed from their wickedness, and renewed by the Holy Ghost.

Expository Thoughts on Luke, 2.33.

No sin seems to be regarded by Christ as more sinful than hypocrisy. None certainly drew forth from his lips such frequent, strong, and withering condemnation, during the whole course of his ministry. He was ever full of mercy and compassion for the chief of sinners. 'Fury was not in him' when he saw Zacchaeus, the penitent thief, Matthew the publican, Saul the persecutor, and the woman in

Simon's house. But when he saw scribes and Pharisees wearing a mere cloak of religion, and pretending to great outward sanctity, while their hearts were full of wickedness, his righteous soul seems to have been full of indignation. Eight times in one chapter (Matt. 23) we find him saying, 'Woe unto you, scribes and Pharisees, hypocrites.'

Expository Thoughts on Luke, 2.258.

Strictness about forms and ceremonies, and utter recklessness about gross sin, are found quite compatible in many hearts.

Expository Thoughts on John, 2.222
(also *Power and Sympathy of Christ,* 124).

IDLENESS

An idle mind is like an open door, and if Satan does not enter in himself by it, it is certain he will throw in something to raise bad thoughts in our souls.

Upper Room, 261.

Everything in the world around us seems to teach the same lesson. It is the still water which becomes stagnant and impure: the running, moving streams are always clear.

Upper Room, 262.

IDOLATRY

Idolatry is a worship, in which the honour due to God in Trinity, and to him only, is given to some of his creatures, or to some invention of his creatures.

Knots Untied, 450.

Beware of manufacturing a God of your own,—a God who is all mercy, but not just,—a God who is all love, but not holy,—a God who has a heaven for everybody, but a hell for none,—a God who can allow good and bad to be side by side in time, but will make no distinction between good and bad in eternity.

Practical Religion, 434.

Novelty is the idol of the day.

Upper Room, 62.

The tendency of these latter days to make an idol of intellect,—the desire to be independent and to think for yourself,—the disposition to worship private judgment, to exalt your own isolated opinion, and to deem it finer and cleverer to go wrong with a few than right with a crowd.

Upper Room, 154.

IGNORANCE

We should notice that a man's heart may be right towards God, while he remains very ignorant of some great doctrines of the Christian faith.

Expository Thoughts on John, 1.295.

Ignorance is universally deplored. But, you may depend, there is no ignorance so common and so mischievous as ignorance of ourselves.

Holiness, 388.

The principal giants whom John Bunyan describes, in 'Pilgrim's Progress,' as dangerous to Christian pilgrims, were two, Pope and

Pagan. If the good old Puritan had foreseen the times we live in, he would have said something about the giant Ignorance.

Practical Religion, 136.

IMPUTATION

Our sins were imputed to him. He was made a curse for us.

Expository Thoughts on John, 1.42.

I believe the 'imputed righteousness of Christ, unto all and upon all them that believe,' is the true garment which remedies the nakedness of the fall (Rom. 3:22.). The indwelling grace of the Spirit is doubtless never separate from that righteousness. But it is in itself a distinct and separate thing, and should be kept distinct in our minds.

Expository Thoughts on Luke, 2.389.

INCARNATION

In a religion which really comes down from heaven there must needs be mysteries. Of such mysteries in Christianity, the incarnation is one.

Expository Thoughts on Luke, 1.21.

INSULTS

There are few things more powerful than ridicule and scorn. It can do far more than open enmity and persecution. Many a man who would march up to a cannon's mouth, or lead a forlorn hope, or storm a breach, has found it impossible to face the mockery of a few companions, and has flinched from the path of duty to avoid it.

Holiness, 188.

ISRAEL

Israel is yet to be gathered. The Jews are yet to be restored to their own land, and to look to him whom they once pierced, as their King and their God. Though the accomplishment of this prediction tarry, we may confidently wait for it. It shall surely come one day and not tarry (Hab. 2:3).

Expository Thoughts on Luke, 1.19.

JERUSALEM

Jerusalem was the wickedest city on earth when our Lord left the world. It was a city which had stoned the prophets and killed those whom God sent to call it to repentance. It was a city full of pride, unbelief, self-righteousness, and desperate hardness of heart. It was a city which had just crowned all its transgressions by crucifying the Lord of glory. And yet Jerusalem was the place at which the first proclamation of repentance and pardon was to be made.—The command of Christ was plain:—'Begin at Jerusalem.'

Expository Thoughts on Luke, 2.386.

JESUS CHRIST

He is God as well as man, and man as well as God.

Knots Untied, 272.

Christ came into the world 'as a Son,' with the keys of God's treasury of grace and truth entirely in his hands (Heb. 3:6). Grace came by him, when he made fully known God's gracious plan of salvation, by faith in his own blood, and opened the fountain of mercy to all the world.

Expository Thoughts on John, 1.26.

Christ is to the souls of men what the sun is to the world. He is the centre and source of all spiritual light, warmth, life, health, growth, beauty, and fertility.

Expository Thoughts on John, 1.10.

There is no sinner too far gone in sin for Christ to raise and convert. He that stood by the grave of Lazarus can say to the vilest of men, 'Come forth: loose him, and let him go.'

Expository Thoughts on John, 2.205
(also *Power and Sympathy of Christ*, 86).

Christ ... did not come on earth to be a conqueror, or a philosopher, or a mere teacher of morality. He came to save sinners. He came to do that which man could never do for himself,—to do that which money and learning can never obtain,—to do that which is essential to man's real happiness: he came to 'take away sin.'

Expository Thoughts on John, 1.40.

Forgotten and despised by the world, perhaps, they are never forgotten by their Saviour. He knows where they dwell, and what their trials are. A book of remembrance is written for them. Their tears are all in his bottle (Psa. 56:8). Their names are graven on the palms of his hands. He notices all they do for him in this evil world, though they think it not worth notice, and he will confess it one day publicly, before his Father and the holy angels.

Expository Thoughts on John, 1.212.

Let all true Christians take comfort in the thought that their Saviour is Lord of waves and winds, of storms and tempests, and can come to them in the darkest hour, 'walking upon the sea.' There are waves of trouble far heavier than any on the Lake of Galilee. There are days of darkness which try the faith of the holiest Christian. But let us never despair if Christ is our Friend. He can come to our aid in an hour when we think not, and in ways that we did not expect. And when he comes, all will be calm.

Expository Thoughts on John, 1.237.

The Captain of our salvation never fails to lead his soldiers to victory. He never makes any useless movements, never errs in judgment, never commits any mistake. His eye is on all his followers, from the greatest of them even to the least. The humblest servant in his army is not forgotten. The weakest and most sickly is cared for, remembered, and kept unto salvation. The souls whom he has purchased and redeemed with his own blood are far too precious to be wasted and thrown away.

Holiness, 84.

In him there is pardon and peace with God, bought by the precious blood which he shed upon the cross. In him there is joy and peace for any believer, and a solid, well-grounded expectation of good things to come. In him there is rest for the weary, refuge for the fearful, a cleansing fountain for the unclean, medicine for the sick, healing for the broken-hearted, and hope for the lost. Whosoever feels labouring and heavy laden with sin, whosoever feels anxious and distressed about his soul, whosoever feels afraid of death and unfit to die,—whosoever he is, *let him go to Christ and trust in him.*

Old Paths, 107.

The keys of death and hell are put in his hand. The government of the gate of heaven is laid on his shoulder. He himself is the door, and

by him all that enter in shall be saved (Acts 5:31; Rev. 1:18; John 10:9).
Old Paths, 176.

The hand that was nailed to the cross is too wise and loving to smite without a needs-be, or to keep us waiting for relief without a cause.
Expository Thoughts on John, 2.169
(also *Power and Sympathy of Christ*, 6).

In him, as our Redeemer and substitute, crucified for our sins and raised again for our justification, there is an endless supply of all that men can need,—pardon, absolution, mercy, grace, peace, rest, relief, comfort, and hope.
Upper Room, 96-97.

The hand of man may take the stone from the grave and show the dead; but none but Jesus can say to the dead, 'Come forth, and live' (John 11:41-43). We must deal directly with Christ.
Upper Room, 97.

Heaven is before us, and Christ the only door into it; hell beneath us, and Christ alone able to deliver from it; the devil behind us, and Christ the only refuge from his wrath and accusations; the law against us, and Christ alone able to redeem us; sin weighing us down, and Christ alone able to put it away.
Knots Untied, 32.

Ascension of Jesus

Our great Head has taken possession of a glorious inheritance in behalf of his mystical body, and holds it as an elder brother and trustee, until the day comes when his body shall be perfected.—As a High Priest, Jesus has gone into heaven to intercede for all who believe on him. There in the holy of holies he presents on their behalf the merit of his own sacrifice, and obtains for them daily supplies of mercy and grace. The grand secret of the perseverance of saints is Christ's appearance for them in heaven. They have an everlasting Advocate with the Father, and therefore they are never cast away (Heb. 9:24; 1 John 2:1).

Expository Thoughts on Luke, 2.391.

Death of Jesus

Christ's death is the Christian's life. Christ's cross is the Christian's title to heaven. Christ 'lifted up' and put to shame on Calvary is the ladder by which Christians 'enter into the holiest,' and are at length landed in glory.

Expository Thoughts on John, 1.102.

Deity of Jesus

The Lord Jesus Christ, the eternal Word, was in nature, essence and substance very God, and that 'as the Father is God, so also the Son is God.'

Expository Thoughts on John, 1.6.

Our Lord's perfect knowledge of all hearts was one among many proofs of his divinity.

Expository Thoughts on John, 1.53.

It would be utterly absurd and untrue to say of any mere man, that at the very time he was speaking to another on earth he was in heaven! But it can be said of Christ with perfect truth and propriety. He never ceased to be very God, when he became incarnate. He was 'with God and was God.' As God, he was in heaven while he was speaking to Nicodemus.

Expository Thoughts on John, 1.108.

High Priest

Jesus is a high priest of perfect *wisdom*. He knows exactly what each of us is, and what each of us requires. 'He will not suffer us to be tempted above that which we are able to bear' (1 Cor. 10:13), nor allow us to remain in the furnace of suffering one moment beyond the time that is required for our refining. He will give us strength according to our day, and grace according to our need. He knows the most secret feelings of our hearts, and understands the meaning of our feeblest prayers.

Upper Room, 193.

He can be touched with a feeling of our infirmities, because he has suffered himself in the body being tempted. He knows by experience all that the body is liable to from pain, and weariness, and hunger, and thirst, and work; and has taken to heaven that very body which endured the contradiction of sinners and was nailed to the tree. Who can doubt that that body in heaven is a continual plea for believers, and renders them ever acceptable in the Father's sight?

Knots Untied, 228.

As a Priest, he offered up his body and soul as a sacrifice for sin upon the cross, and made a complete atonement for us with his own blood. As a Priest, he ascended up on high, passed within the veil, and entered into the presence of God. As a Priest, he is now sitting on our behalf at the right hand of God; and what he began actively on earth he is carrying on actively in heaven. That is what Christ is doing.

Knots Untied, 277.

Christ is a High Priest of almighty *power*. There is no sin that he cannot pardon, and no sinner that he cannot absolve.

Knots Untied, 298.

To whom should the sick man disclose his ailment, but the physician?

To whom should the prisoner tell his story, but to his legal advocate? To whom should the sinner open his heart and confess his sins, but to him who is the 'advocate with the father, Jesus Christ the righteous'? (1 John 2:1).

Knots Untied, 298-99.

Humanity of Jesus

He knows what sorrow is, for he was a Man of sorrows. He knows what an aching body is, for his body was racked with pain. He cried, 'All my bones are out of joint' (Psa. 22:14). He knows what poverty and weariness are, for he was often wearied and had not where to lay his head. He knows what family unkindness is, for even his brethren did not believe him. He had no honour in his own house.

Holiness, 427.

Humility of Jesus

From his cradle to his grave he was 'clothed with humility' (1 Pet. 5:5). He was born of a poor woman, and spent the first thirty years of his life in a carpenter's house at Nazareth. He was followed by poor companions,—many of them no better than fishermen. He was poor in his manner of living: 'The foxes [had] holes, and the birds of the air nests; but the Son of man [had] not where to lay his head' (Matt. 8:20). When he went on the Sea of Galilee, it was in a borrowed boat; hen he rode into Jerusalem, it was on a borrowed ass; when he was buried, it was in a borrowed tomb. 'Though he was rich, yet for [our] sakes he became poor' (2 Cor. 8:9).

Expository Thoughts on John, 1.235.

Incarnation

Next to the doctrine of the Trinity, there is no doctrine on which fallen man has built so many deadly heresies as the incarnation of Christ.

Expository Thoughts on John, 1.21.

Intercession

As soon as the blood of the great Sacrifice began to flow, the great High Priest began to intercede.

Expository Thoughts on Luke, 2.348.

We ought to remember that he is now sitting on the right hand of God, to do a work as real, as true, as important to our souls, as the work which he did when he shed his blood.

Old Paths, 416.

What is the value of that bank note without the signature? Nothing at all. Once get a few words, a very few letters, traced in ink upon the corner of that bank note, and that which was a piece of waste paper a few moments before, becomes worth, it may be, many hundred pounds, through the signature being attached to it. So it is with the intercession of Christ. He signs, endorses, and presents the believer's petitions; and through his all-prevailing intercession they are heard on high, and bring down blessings upon the Christian's soul.

Old Paths, 423.

Let us carefully remark that our Lord never changes. He did not leave behind him his human nature when he ascended up into heaven. At this moment, at God's right hand, he can be touched with the feeling of our infirmities and can understand tears as well as ever. Our great High Priest is the very Friend that our souls need, able to save as God, able to feel as man.

Expository Thoughts on John, 2.199
(also *Power and Sympathy of Christ,* 72-73).

Love for Jesus

Once let a man see the full meaning of the words, 'Christ loved me and gave himself for me,' and then he will delight to give himself to Christ, and all that he has to his service.

Practical Religion, 314.

You might as well take away the sun out of heaven, as take away the name of Christ from believers. To the world there may seem little in his name. To believers it is full of comfort, hope, joy, rest, and peace.

Christmas Thoughts, 57.

Love of Jesus

Christ's lovingkindness to his people never changes, and never fails. It is a deep well, of which no one ever found the bottom. It began from all eternity, before they were born. It chose, called, and quickened them when they were dead in trespasses and sins. It drew them to God and changed their character, and put a new will in their minds, and a new song in their mouths. It has borne with them in all their waywardness and shortcomings. It will never allow them to be separated from God. It will flow ever forward, like a mighty river, through the endless ages of eternity. Christ's love and mercy must be a sinner's plea when he first begins his journey. Christ's love and mercy will be his only plea when he crosses the dark river and enters home. Let us seek to know this love by inward experience, and prize it more. Let it constrain us more continually to live, not to ourselves, but to him who died for us and rose again.

Expository Thoughts on Luke, 1.111.

The Lord Jesus is indeed most pitiful, most compassionate, most gracious. None are too wicked for him to care for. None are too far gone in sin for his almighty heart to take interest about their souls. He wept over unbelieving Jerusalem. He heard the prayer of the dying thief. He stopped under the tree to call the publican Zacchaeus. He came down from heaven to turn the heart of the persecutor Saul. He found time to pray for his murderers even on the cross. Love like this is a love that passeth knowledge.

Expository Thoughts on Luke, 2.345-46.

There is no end to his compassion: there are no bounds to his pity. He is not ashamed to befriend those whom the world casts off as hopeless. There are none too bad, too filthy, and too much diseased with sin, to be admitted into his home. He is willing to be the friend of any sinner: he has kindness and mercy and healing medicine for all.

Practical Religion, 323.

We love where we can give some reason for loving: the great Friend of sinners draws his reasons out of his own everlasting compassion.

Practical Religion, 323.

There are degrees of grace, and varieties of grace; but the least, the weakest, the feeblest disciples, are all loved by the Lord Jesus. Then let no believer's heart fail because of his infirmities and, above all, let no believer dare to despise and undervalue a brother.

Expository Thoughts on John, 2.168
(also *Power and Sympathy of Christ,* 4).

His love never changes: ours is wavering and uncertain.

Expository Thoughts on John, 2.174
(also *Power and Sympathy of Christ,* 18).

Every true Christian has a Friend in heaven, of almighty power and boundless love. He is thought of, cared for, provided for, defended by God's eternal Son. He has an unfailing Protector, who never slumbers or sleeps, and watches continually over his interests.

Expository Thoughts on John, 2.178
(also *Power and Sympathy of Christ,* 27).

Mediator

All men ought to think of Christ, because of *the office Christ fills between God and man*. He is the eternal Son of God, through whom alone the Father can be known, approached, and served. He is the appointed mediator between God and man, through whom alone we can be reconciled with God, pardoned, justified, and saved. He is the divine person whom God the Father has sealed to be the giver of everything that man requires for his soul. To him are committed the keys of death and hell. In his favour is life. In him alone there is hope of salvation for mankind. Without him no child of Adam can be saved.

Christmas Thoughts, 34.

Natures (Hypostatic Union)

This union of two natures in Christ's one Person is doubtless one of the greatest mysteries of the Christian religion. It needs to be carefully stated. It is just one of those great truths which are not meant to be curiously pried into, but to be reverently believed.

Expository Thoughts on John, 1.18.

Resurrection of Jesus

Let no one misunderstand my meaning. I do not say that we dwell too much on the sacrifice and the blood of Christ, but I do contend that we dwell too little on his resurrection.

Upper Room, 9.

When our Lord rose again from the dead, he rose with a real human body,—a body which could not be in two places at once,—a body of which the angels said, 'He is not here, but he is risen' (Luke 24:6). In that body, having finished his redeeming work on earth, he ascended visibly into heaven. He took his body with him, and did not leave it behind, like Elijah's mantle.

Knots Untied, 227.

Second Adam

The second Adam is far greater than the first Adam was. The first Adam was only man, and so he fell. The second Adam was God as well as man, and so he completely conquered.

Expository Thoughts on John, 1.19.

Heaven, in a spiritual sense shut by the sin of the first Adam, would be opened by the obedience of the second Adam.

Expository Thoughts on John, 1.61.

Second Coming

To attend a marriage feast, and cleanse the temple from profanation were among the first acts of our Lord's ministry at his first coming. To purify the whole visible church, and hold a marriage supper, will be among his first acts, when he comes again.

Expository Thoughts on John, 1.73-74.

The second coming of Christ shall be utterly unlike the first. He came the first time in weakness, a tender infant, born of a poor woman in the manger at Bethlehem, unnoticed, unhonoured, and scarcely known. He shall come the second time in royal dignity, with the armies of heaven around him, to be known, recognized, and feared, by all the tribes of the earth. He came the first time to suffer,—to bear our sins, to be reckoned a curse, to be despised, rejected, unjustly condemned, and slain. He shall come the second time to reign,—to put down every enemy beneath his feet, to take the kingdoms of this world for his inheritance, to rule them with righteousness, to judge all men, and to live for evermore.

Expository Thoughts on Mark, 226.

A day is coming on the earth when the long-suffering of God towards sinners shall have an end. The door of mercy, which has been so long open, shall at last be shut. The fountain opened for all sin and uncleanness shall at length be closed. The throne of grace shall be removed, and the throne of judgment shall be set up in its place. The great assize of the world shall begin. All that are found impenitent and unbelieving shall be thrust out forever from God's presence. Men shall find that there is such a thing as 'the wrath of the Lamb' (Rev. 6:16).

Expository Thoughts on Luke, 2.100.

The world will not be converted when Jesus comes again. The earth will not be full of the knowledge of the Lord. The reign of peace will not have been established. The millennium will not have begun. These glorious things will come to pass *after* the second advent, but not before.

Expository Thoughts on Luke, 2.182.

The day of Christ's second advent shall be the day when good and evil, converted and unconverted, shall at length be divided into two distinct bodies. The visible church shall no longer be a mixed body. The wheat and the tares shall no longer grow side by side. The good fish and the bad shall at length be sorted into two bodies. The angels shall come forth, and gather together the godly, that they may be rewarded; and leave the wicked behind to be punished.

Expository Thoughts on Luke, 2.184.

The Great High Priest is yet to come forth from the Holy of Holies, to bless all the people who have believed on him. *One* part of his work he did when he died upon the cross; *another* part of his work he is still doing,—interceding for us at God's right hand. But the *third* part of the High Priest's office remains yet to be done. He has yet to come forth from the Holy of Holies, as the high-priest did upon the day of atonement,—to come forth from within the veil to bless the people.

Old Paths, 427-28.

The world has not yet seen the last of him.

Practical Religion, 17.

Those who would not move when they heard the church-going bell, shall obey the voice of the archangel and the trump of God.

Christmas Thoughts, 36.

Substitution

Christ has *stood in the place* of the true Christian. He has become his Surety and his Substitute. He undertook to bear all that was to be borne, and to do all that was to be done, and what he undertook he performed. Hence the true Christian is a justified man (Isa. 53:6).

Old Paths, 207.

Sympathy of Jesus for Children

Our Lord is able to sympathize with man in every stage of man's existence, from the cradle to the grave. He knows by experience the nature and temperament of the child, the boy, and the young man. He has stood in their place. He has occupied their position. He knows their hearts. Let us never forget this in dealing with young people about their souls. Let us tell them confidently, that there is One in heaven at the right hand of God, who is exactly suited to be their Friend. He who died on the cross was once a boy himself, and feels a special interest in boys and girls, as well as in grown-up people.

Expository Thoughts on Luke, 1.59.

Union with Christ

They that live unto the Lord are generally the only people who die in the Lord.

Holiness, 57.

It is possible to have 'union' with Christ, and yet to have little if any 'communion' with him.

Holiness, 127.

The grand secret of communion with Christ is to be continually 'living the life of faith in him,' and drawing out of him every hour the supply that every hour requires.

Practical Religion, 15.

JOHN THE BAPTIST

He claims honour not for himself but for Christ. To exalt Christ was his mission, and to that mission he steadfastly adheres.

The greatest saints of God in every age of the church have always been men of John the Baptist's spirit.

Expository Thoughts on John, 1.31.

JOY

A cheerful, kindly spirit is a great recommendation to a believer. It is a positive misfortune to Christianity when a Christian cannot smile.

Expository Thoughts on John, 1.64.

JUDGING

We must beware of making the experience of other believers the measure of our own. We must beware of denying another's grace, because he has not been led by the same way as ourselves.

Expository Thoughts on John, 1.42.

Let us be more quick to see grace and more slow to see imperfections!

Holiness, 274.

JUDGMENT

A day will come when those who are not born again will wish that they had never been born at all.

Expository Thoughts on John, 1.88.

Although man's salvation is entirely of God, his ruin, if he is lost, will be entirely from himself. He will reap the fruit of his own sowing.

Expository Thoughts on John, 1.103.

There is a day coming when the Lord Jesus Christ shall judge his people, and give to every one according to his works. The course of this world shall not always go on as it does now. Disorder, confusion, false profession, and unpunished sin, shall not always cover the face of the earth. The great white throne shall be set up. The Judge of all shall sit upon it. The dead shall be raised from their graves. The living shall all be summoned to the bar. The books shall be opened. High and low, rich and poor, gentle and simple, all shall at length give account to God, and all shall receive an eternal sentence.

Expository Thoughts on Luke, 2.223-24.

JUSTIFICATION

The very moment a sinner believes on Christ he is justified and accepted. There is no condemnation for him. He has peace with God, and that immediately and without delay. His name is in the book of life, however little he may be aware of it. He has a title to heaven, which death and hell and Satan can not overthrow. Happy are those who know this truth! It is an essential part of the good news of the gospel.

Expository Thoughts on John, 1.268.

'We conclude that a man is justified by faith without the deeds of the law' (Rom. 3:20-28) The only righteousness in which we can appear before God is the righteousness of another—even the perfect righteousness of our Substitute and Representative, Jesus Christ the Lord. His work, and not our work, is our only title to heaven.

Holiness, 30.

The expression, 'is not condemned,' is equivalent to saying, 'he is pardoned, acquitted, justified, cleared from all guilt, delivered from the curse of a broken law, no longer counted a sinner, but reckoned perfectly righteous in the sight of God.'

Expository Thoughts on John, 1.114-15.

Tried by the perfect standard of God's law the best of Christians is nothing better than a justified sinner, a pardoned criminal.

Old Paths, 206.

Justification and Sanctification

Our justification is a perfect finished work, and admits of no degrees. Our sanctification is imperfect and incomplete, and will be so to the last hour of our life.

Holiness, 159.

Justification is the *reckoning* and counting a man to be righteous for the sake of another, even Jesus Christ the Lord. Sanctification is the actual *making* a man inwardly righteous, though it may be in a very feeble degree.

Holiness, 41.

There are degrees in our sanctification. In our justification there are none.

Holiness, 146.

I am inclined to think that justification and sanctification are insensibly confused together in the minds of many believers. They receive the gospel truth—that there must be something done in us, as well as something done for us, if we are true members of Christ: and so far they are right. But then, without being aware of it, perhaps, they seem to imbibe the idea that their justification is, in some degree, affected by something within themselves. They do not clearly see that Christ's work, not their own work—either in whole or in part, either directly or indirectly—is alone the ground of our acceptance with God; that justification is a thing entirely without us, for which nothing whatever is needful on our part but simple faith—and that the weakest believer is as fully and completely justified as the strongest.

Holiness, 158-59.

KINGDOM OF GOD

By the terms of the everlasting covenant, the Father has given to the Son power over all flesh, to quicken whom he will,—to justify, to sanctify, to keep, and to glorify his people,—to judge, and finally punish the wicked and unbelieving,—and at last to take to himself a kingdom over all the world, and put down every enemy under his feet.

Expository Thoughts on John, 1.132.

The kingdom of God is the only kingdom worth labouring for. All other kingdoms shall, sooner or later, decay and pass away. The statesmen who rear them are like men who build houses of cards, or children, who make palaces of sand on the sea shore. The wealth which constitutes their greatness is as liable to melt away as the snow in spring. The kingdom of God is the only kingdom which shall endure for ever.

Expository Thoughts on Luke, 2.60.

['The kingdom of God is within you.'] This expression again is interpreted two ways. Some hold with our translators, that the word 'within' means, 'in your hearts and consciences. The kingdom of God is an inward and spiritual thing, and not an external and visible thing.'—Others hold with our marginal reading, that 'within,' means 'among you.' The kingdom has already begun in the midst of your nation. My disciples have already joined it and become its first subjects. While you are waiting, my spiritual kingdom has already been set up. I decidedly adhere to this last view.

Expository Thoughts on Luke, 2.180.

KNOWLEDGE

To know the root of a disease is one step towards a remedy. He that is forewarned is forearmed.

Holiness, 207.

The moment a man begins to think he knows better than God, and that God does not mean anything when he threatens, his soul is in great danger. When we cannot see the reason of God's dealings, our duty is to hold our peace and believe.

Holiness, 225.

As a great divine said on his deathbed, 'We are all of us only half awake.' The best Christian among us knows but little of his glorious Saviour, even after he had learned to believe. We see through a glass darkly. We do not realize the 'unsearchable riches' there are in him. When we wake up after his likeness in another world, we shall be amazed that we knew him so imperfectly, and loved him so little.

Holiness, 389-90.

LATIMER, HUGH

The history of Latimer's episcopate is short and simple, for it only lasted four years. He was the same man in a bishop's palace that he had been in a country parsonage, or a Cambridge pulpit. Promotion did not spoil him. The mitre did not prove an extinguisher to his zeal for the gospel.

Light from Old Times, 134.

He did not shrink from attacking anybody's sins, even if they were the sins of a king. When Henry VIII checked the diffusion of the Bible, Latimer wrote him a plain-spoken letter, long before he was a bishop, remonstrating with him on his conduct. He feared God, and nothing else did he fear. 'Latimer, Latimer', he exclaimed at the beginning of one of his sermons, 'thou art going to speak before the high and mighty King Henry VIII, who is able, if he think fit, to take thy life away. Be careful what thou sayest. But Latimer, Latimer, remember also thou art about to speak before the King of kings and Lord of lords. Take heed that thou dost not displease him.'

Light from Old Times, 143-44.

LAW

The honour of God's holy law was frequently defended by Christ during the time of his ministry on earth. Sometimes we find him defending it against man-made additions, as in the case of the fourth commandment. Sometimes we find him defending it against those who would lower the standard of its requirements, and allow it to be transgressed, as in the case of the law of marriage. But never do we find him speaking of the law in any terms but those of respect.

Expository Thoughts on Luke, 2.155.

Its ceremonial part was a type of his own gospel, and was to be fulfilled to the last letter. Its moral part was a revelation of God's eternal mind, and was to be perpetually binding on Christians.

Expository Thoughts on Luke, 2.155-56.

There is not a commandment in all the ten which does not condemn us. If we have not broken it in deed we have in word; if we have not broken it in word, we have in thought and imagination,—and that continually. Tried by the standard of the fifth chapter of St Matthew, there is not one of us that would be acquitted.

Old Paths, 170.

LEGALISM

It is a bad symptom of any man's state of soul, when he begins to put the second things in religion in the first place, and the first things in the second, or the things ordained by man above the things ordained by God. Let us beware of falling into this state of mind. There is something sadly wrong in our spiritual condition, when the only thing we look at in others is their outward Christianity, and the principal question we ask is, whether they worship in our communion, and use our ceremonial, and serve God in our way.—Do they repent of sin? Do they believe on Christ? Are they living holy lives? These are the chief points to which our attention ought to be directed. The moment we begin to place anything in religion before these things, we are in danger of becoming as thorough Pharisees as the accusers of the disciples.

Expository Thoughts on Luke, 1.123.

LIBERALISM

I have often been told that 'broad' views are wanted in the present day. I wish to be as broad as the Bible, neither less nor more. I say that he is the narrow-minded theologian, who pares down such parts of the Bible as the natural heart dislikes, and rejects any portion of the counsel of God.

Holiness, 236.

Preach salvation by the sacraments, exalt the church above Christ, and keep back the doctrine of the atonement, and the devil cares little,—his goods are at peace.

Old Paths, 179.

It was well and truly said that in those ancient days 'the Church had wooden communion vessels, but golden ministers,' and it was this which gave the primitive Church its power. And when religion began to decay, it was said that the conditions were reversed; the ministers became wooden and the communion plate golden.

Charges and Addresses, 107.

A wave of extravagant liberalism in religion, as well as in everything else, is sweeping over England. Concerning the Trinity, the Divinity of Christ, the atonement, the person and work of the Holy Ghost, conversion, justification, the inspiration of Scripture, the future state, and the like, it seems to be agreed that men may believe as much or as little as they please, and nobody is to find fault.

Charges and Addresses, 149.

Loose, vague, misty, broad Christianity may avoid offence and please people in health and prosperity, but it will not convert souls, or supply solid comfort in the hour of sorrow or sickness, or on the bed of death.

Upper Room, 200.

If men and women can be saved without repentance, faith, and holiness, we may as well throw the Bible away, and give up Christianity altogether.

Upper Room, 202.

From the liberality which says everybody is right, from the charity which forbids us to say anybody is wrong, from the piece which is bought at the expense of truth,—may the good Lord deliver us!

Knots Untied, 45.

LIBERTY

Each must know his own strength and natural temperament, and act accordingly. One believer can go without risk where another cannot. Happy is he who can use his Christian liberty without abusing it!

Expository Thoughts on John, 1.65.

LIES

Lying is just one of the sins to which the human heart is most naturally inclined, and one of the commonest sins in the world. Gehazi, Ananias, and Sapphira have more followers and imitators than Peter and Paul.

Expository Thoughts on Luke, 2.40.

LONGSUFFERING

It is evident that our Lord condemns everything like a revengeful, pugnacious, litigious, or quarrelsome spirit. He forbids everything like duelling, or fighting, between individuals, for the settlement of private wrongs. He enjoins forbearance, patience, and long-suffering under injuries and insults. He would have us concede much, submit to much, and put up with much, rather than cause strife. He would have us endure much inconvenience and loss, and even sacrifice some of our just rights, rather than have any contention.

Expository Thoughts on Luke, 1.144.

LORD'S SUPPER

Sinners living in open sin, and determined not to give it up, ought on no account to come to the Lord's table. To do so is a positive insult to Christ, and to pour contempt on his gospel. It is nonsense to profess we desire to remember Christ's death, while we cling to the accursed thing which made it needful for Christ to die.

Practical Religion, 136.

To suppose that Christ's ordinances can do good to an unspiritual man, is as foolish as to put bread and wine into the mouth of a dead person.

Practical Religion, 138.

Does a man truly repent of sin and hate it? Does a man put his trust in Jesus Christ as his only hope of salvation? Does a man live in charity towards others? He that can truly say to each of these questions, 'I do,' he is a man that is scripturally qualified for the Lord's supper. Let him come boldly.

Practical Religion, 139.

The Lord's supper was not intended for unsinning angels, but for men and women compassed with infirmity, dwelling in a world full of temptations, and needing mercy and grace every day they live.

Practical Religion, 146-47.

Justification is not by the sacraments. To eat the bread and drink the wine is not the way to obtain forgiveness of sins or converting grace.

Upper Room, 374.

A communicant was not expected to be an angel, but a sinner who feels his sins, and trusts in his Saviour.

Knots Untied, 202.

Eating the bread with faith, he feels closer communion with the body of Christ. Drinking the wine with faith, he feels closer communion with the blood of Christ. He sees more clearly what Christ is to him, and what he is to Christ. He understands more thoroughly what it is to be one with Christ and Christ with him. He feels the roots of his spiritual life insensibly watered, and the work of grace within him insensibly built up and carried forward. He cannot explain or define it. It is a matter of experience, which no one knows but he who feels it. And the true expression of the whole matter is this,—there is a special and spiritual 'presence' of Christ in the ordinance of the Lord's Supper. Jesus meets those who draw near to his Table with a true heart, in a special and peculiar way.

Knots Untied, 223.

Transubstantiation

Hundreds of clergy, both in high places and low, consider that there is not only a real presence of Christ in the Lord's Supper, which I hold as strongly as they do, but that there is also a real presence of Christ in the elements of bread and wine after consecration, which I entirely deny.

Knots Untied, 189-90.

Not one of the writers of the New Testament ever speaks of the sacrament as a sacrifice, or calls the Lord's table an altar, or even hints that a Christian minister is a sacrificing priest. The universal doctrine of the New Testament is that after the one offering of Christ there remains no more need of sacrifice.

Practical Religion, 134.

If the body of him who was born of the Virgin Mary can be present in the bread and wine on the Lord's table, it cannot be a true human body, and the comfortable truth that our Saviour is *perfect man* would be overthrown. Those who tell us that as soon as the words of consecration are pronounced, at once the body and blood of Christ come down into the bread and wine, are in great error, and assert what they cannot prove.

Upper Room, 377.

No doubt it may satisfy such controversialists as the late Cardinal Wiseman to adduce such texts as 'This is my body', and 'This is my blood', as proofs that the Lord's Supper is a sacrifice. But a man must be easily satisfied if such texts content him. The quotation of a single isolated phrase is a mode of arguing that would establish Arianism or Socinianism.

Knots Untied, 187.

LOVE

Love to Christ is the infallible mark of all true children of God.

Expository Thoughts on John, 2.85.

Let us observe that of all graces, love is the one which most arrests the attention and influences the opinion of the world.

Expository Thoughts on John, 2.201
(also *Power and Sympathy of Christ*, 79).

Faith will one day be swallowed up in sight, and hope in certainty. Their office will be useless in the morning of the resurrection, and like old almanacs, they will be laid aside. But love will live on through the endless ages of eternity.

Practical Religion, 167.

Where there is no love there is no spiritual life.

Upper Room, 87.

Love for Jesus

All desire to see among Christians, more good works, more self-denial, more practical obedience to Christ's commands. But what will produce these things? Nothing, nothing but love. There never will be more done for Christ till there is more hearty love to Christ himself. The fear of punishment, the desire of reward, the sense of duty, are all useful arguments, in their way, to persuade men to holiness. But they are all weak and powerless, until a man loves Christ. Once let that mighty principle get hold of a man, and you will see his whole life changed.

Expository Thoughts on Luke, 1.181.

Love of Neighbour

We must love all men, and be kind to all, whenever occasion requires.

Expository Thoughts on Luke, 1.287.

MARRIAGE

Marriage is not a sacrament, as the Church of Rome asserts. It is simply a state of life ordained by God for man's benefit.

Expository Thoughts on John, 1.63.

Society is never in a healthy condition, and true religion never flourishes, in that land where the marriage tie is lightly esteemed.

Expository Thoughts on John, 1.63.

Too many seem to think of everything except religion in choosing a partner for life, or to suppose that it will come somehow as a matter of course. Yet when a praying, Bible-reading, God-fearing, Christ-loving, Sabbath-keeping Christian marries a person who takes no interest whatever in serious religion, what can the result be but injury to the Christian, or immense unhappiness? Health is not infectious, but disease is.

Practical Religion, 283.

MEANS OF GRACE

We must labour in the use of all appointed means. We must read our Bibles, like men digging for hidden treasure. We must wrestle earnestly in prayer, like men contending with a deadly enemy for life. We must take our whole heart to the house of God, and worship and hear like those who listen to the reading of a will. We must fight daily against sin, the world, and the devil, like those who fight for liberty, and must conquer or be slaves. These are the ways we must walk in if we would find Christ, and be found of him.

Expository Thoughts on John, 1.244.

Means of grace are not to be despised because they are not saviours. Gold is not food; you cannot eat it,—but you would not therefore say it is useless, and throw it away. Your soul's eternal well-doing most certainly does not depend on means of grace, but it is no less certain that without them, as a general rule, your soul will not do well. God *might* take all who are saved to heaven in a chariot of fire, as he did Elijah, but he does not do so. He *might* teach them all by visions, and dreams, and miraculous interpositions, without requiring them to read or think for themselves, but he does not do so. And why not? Because he is a God that works by means, and it is his law and will that in all man's dealings with him means shall be used.

Thoughts for Young Men, 63-64.

MERCY

What are we doing to help those who are troubled in mind, body, or estate? There are many such in this world. There are always some near our own doors. What are we doing for them?

Expository Thoughts on Luke, 1.289.

MESSIAH

It is a grave mistake to suppose that holy men and women under the Old Testament knew nothing about the sacrifice which Christ was to offer up for the sin of the world. Their light, no doubt, was far less clear than ours. They saw things afar off and indistinctly, which we see, as it were, close at hand. But there is not the slightest proof that any Old Testament saint ever looked to any other satisfaction for sin, but that which God promised to make by sending Messiah. From Abel downwards the whole company of old believers appear to have been ever resting on a promised sacrifice, and a blood of almighty efficacy yet to be revealed. From the beginning of the world there has never been but one foundation of hope and peace for sinners—the death of an almighty Mediator between God and man. That foundation is the centre truth of all revealed religion. It was the subject of which Moses and Elijah were seen speaking when they appeared in glory.—They spoke of the atoning death of Christ.

Expository Thoughts on Luke, 1.241-42.

Christ was the substance of every Old Testament sacrifice, ordained in the law of Moses. Christ was the true Deliverer and King, of whom all the judges and deliverers in Jewish history were types. Christ was the coming Prophet greater than Moses, whose glorious advent filled the pages of prophets. Christ was the true seed of the woman who was to bruise the serpent's head,—the true seed in whom all nations were to be blessed,—the true Shiloh to whom the people were to be gathered,—the true scapegoat,—the true brazen serpent,—the true Lamb to which every daily offering pointed,—the true High Priest of whom every descendant of Aaron was a figure. These things, or something like them, we need not doubt, were some of the things which our Lord expounded in the way to Emmaus.

Expository Thoughts on Luke, 2.373.

MINISTERS

He is not a mediator between God and man. He has no power to put away sin, or impart grace. His whole business is to receive the bread of life which his Master provides, and to distribute it among the souls among whom he labours. He cannot make men value the bread, or receive it. He cannot make it soul-saving, or life-giving, to anyone. This is not his work. For this he is not responsible. His whole business is to be a faithful distributor of the food which his divine Master has provided; and that done, his office is discharged.

Expository Thoughts on John, 1.228-29.

Would we know whether a minister is sound in the faith, and deserving of our confidence as a teacher? We have only to ask a simple question, Where is Christ in his teaching?—Would we know whether we ourselves are receiving benefit from the preaching we attend? Let us ask whether its effect is to magnify Christ in our esteem? A minister who is really doing us good will make us think more of Jesus every year we live.

Expository Thoughts on Luke, 1.74

The man who teaches the same doctrine that Christ taught cannot be wrong.

Holiness, 237.

A minister must not despair, and accuse himself of unfaithfulness, because the gospel he preaches is not honoured in his own congregation, and many remain hardened and unbelieving, after he has preached to them many years. Let him remember that he is sharing his Master's lot.

Expository Thoughts on John, 1.181.

We should make up our minds to expect to find spiritual darkness the rule, and spiritual light the exception. Few things in the long run give so much trouble to ministers, missionaries, teachers, and district-visitors, as beginning work with extravagant and unscriptural expectations.

Expository Thoughts on John, 1.104.

Let us settle it in our minds that the ministerial office is *a most wise and useful provision of God.* It secures the regular maintenance of all Christ's ordinances and means of grace. It provides an undying machinery for promoting the awakening of sinners and the edification of saints. All experience proves that everybody's business soon becomes nobody's business; and if this is true in other matters, it is no less true in the matter of religion. Our God is a God of order, and a God who works by means, and we have no right to expect his cause to be kept up by constant miraculous interpositions, while his servants stand idle. For the uninterrupted preaching of the Word and administration of the sacraments, no better plan can be devised than the appointment of a regular order of men who shall give themselves wholly to Christ's business.

Holiness, 381.

The minister who neglects the sick members of his flock is no true pastor. He must not be surprised if people say that he cares for the fleece of his sheep more than for their health.

Expository Thoughts on Luke, 1.222

Do we desire to help forward the cause of pure and undefiled religion in the world? Then let us never forget to pray for ministers, and especially for young men about to enter the ministry. The progress of the gospel, under God, will always depend much on the character and conduct of those who profess to preach it. An unconverted minister can never be expected to do good to souls. He cannot teach properly what he does not feel experimentally. From such men let us pray daily that the church may be delivered. Converted ministers are God's special gift. Man cannot create them. If we would have good ministers, we must remember our Lord's example, and pray for them. Their work is heavy. Their responsibility is enormous. Their strength is small. Let us see that we support them, and hold up their hands by our prayers.

Expository Thoughts on Luke, 1.131-32.

It is a solemn thing to be a minister of the gospel. It is a painful thing to look on, and notice the ways of mankind in spiritual matters. We hold in our hands that great statute Book of God, which declares that without repentance, and conversion, and faith in Christ, and holiness, no man living can be saved. In discharge of our office we urge men to repent, believe, and be saved; but, alas, how frequently we have to lament that our labour seems all in vain. Men attend our churches, and listen, and approve, but do not 'strive' to be saved. We show the sinfulness of sin; we unfold the loveliness of Christ; we expose the vanity of the world; we set forth the happiness of Christ's service; we offer the living water to the wearied and heavy laden sons of toil: but, alas, how often we seem to speak to the winds.

Practical Religion, 31.

We must talk to our people when we are out of church, if we would understand how to preach to them in the church.

Simplicity in Preaching, 21.

Let us ask him who holds the stars in his right hand to revive his work among our ministers, and to raise up men for our times. He can do it. He is willing to do it. He waits to be entreated. Then let all who pray cry night and day to the Lord of the harvest, 'Lord, send forth more labourers into thy harvest.'

Christian Leaders of the Eighteenth Century, 409.

Honour your minister as a faithful ambassador of Christ. Esteem him very highly in love for his work's sake. But never forget that *infallibility is not to be found in godly ministers, but in the Bible.*

Knots Untied, 413-14.

The Goal of Ministers

Let there be no mistake as to the object which true ministers of the gospel have in view. We are not set apart merely to perform a certain round of ordinances,—to read prayers, to baptize those that are baptized, to bury those that are buried, to marry those that are married. We are set apart for the grand purpose of proclaiming the one true living way, and inviting you to walk in it.

Old Paths, 412.

Ministerial Burnout

I firmly believe that one reason why the health of hard-working clergymen so frequently fails, is the great difficulty they find in getting a day of rest. I am sure, if the body could tell its wants, it would cry loudly, 'Remember the Sabbath Day.'

Charges and Addresses, 318.

Ministerial Disagreements

Let us believe that many Churchman with whom we now disagree, may be, and often are, real Christians, in spite of all their errors. Their hearts may be right in the sight of God, though their heads seem to us very wrong. However erroneous we may consider their views, we must charitably hope that they are in the way of life and travelling toward heaven, and will be 'saved by the grace of God, even as ourselves.'

Charges and Addresses, 266.

Pastoral Visitation

To secure the sympathy and personal affection of parishioners is one great secret of ministerial usefulness. Thousands of people care little for eloquent sermons and powerful addresses, addressed to large crowds in which they form nothing better than an insignificant unit. The way to their hearts is to be found by going to their houses, sitting down by their side, taking them by the hand, dealing with them individually as friends, and exhibiting a brotherly interest in their sorrows and their joys.

Charges and Addresses, 109.

It was a true saying of that wise man, Dr Chalmers, that 'a house-going minister makes a church-going people.'

Charges and Addresses, 110.

Double and redouble regular, patient house-to-house visitation. Gather together young men, and deal kindly and genially with them. Invite in all matters the aid of your steady, godly laymen, and let them see that you think them as much a part of the Church as yourselves. Lift up the Lord Jesus Christ in your pulpits, in all his offices, as lovingly, plainly, and in as simple Saxon as you possibly can.

Charges and Addresses, 282.

Unconverted Ministers

An unconverted minister is an injury and burden to a church. How can a man speak of truths which he has never tasted? How can he testify of a Saviour whom he has never seen by faith, and never laid hold on for his own soul? The pastor after God's own heart, is a man to whom the word of God has come. He runs confidently, because he has tidings. He speaks boldly, because he has been sent.

Expository Thoughts on Luke, 1.66.

Learning, and rank, and high ecclesiastical office are no proof that a minister is taught by the Spirit.

Expository Thoughts on John, 1.100.

A false minister may say, 'You have no right to use your private judgment: leave the Bible to us who are ordained.' A true minister will say, 'Search the Scriptures, and if I do no teach you what is scriptural, do not believe me.' A false minister may cry, 'Hear the church,' and 'Hear me.' A true minister will say, 'Hear the Word of God.'

Practical Religion, 111.

The celebrated lawyer, Blackstone, had the curiosity, early in the reign of George III, to go from church to church and hear every clergyman of note in London. He says that he did not hear a single discourse which had more Christianity in it than the writings of Cicero, and that it would have been impossible for him to discover, from what he heard, whether the preacher were a follower of Confucius, of Mahomet, or of Christ!

Christian Leaders of the Eighteenth Century, 5.

They neither did good themselves, nor liked anyone else to do it for them. They hunted, they shot, they farmed, they swore, they drank, they gambled. They seemed determined to know everything except Jesus Christ and him crucified. When they assembled it was generally to toast 'Church and King', and to build one another up in earthly-mindedness, prejudice, ignorance, and formality. When they retired to their own homes, it was to do as little and preach as seldom as possible. And when they did preach, their sermons were so unspeakably and indescribably bad, that it is comforting to reflect they were generally preached to empty benches.

Christian Leaders of the Eighteenth Century, 7
(describing the state of clergy in the eighteenth century).

MIRACLES

Five things should always be noted about our Lord's miracles. 1. Their *number*: they were not a few only but, very many indeed. 2. Their *greatness*: they were not little, but mighty interferences with the ordinary course of nature. 3. Their *publicity*: they were generally not done in a corner, but in open day, and before many witnesses, and often before enemies. 4. Their *character*: they were almost always works of love, mercy, and compassion, helpful and beneficial to man and not mere barren exhibitions of power. 5. Their *direct appeal to men's senses*: they were visible, and would bear any examination.

Expository Thoughts on John, 1.217.

'This man,' they said, 'doeth many miracles' (John 11:47). The facts which wise men pretend to deny now, no one pretended to deny eighteen hundred years ago.

Expository Thoughts on John, 1.213.

He that denies Old Testament miracles, is assaulting the knowledge and veracity of Christ and the apostles. They believed them, and spoke of them, as historical facts. We never need be ashamed of being on their side.

Expository Thoughts on John, 1.255.

Let us beware of supposing that miracles alone have any power to convert men's souls, and to make them Christians. The idea is a complete delusion. To fancy, as some do, that if they saw something wonderful done before their eyes in confirmation of the gospel, they would at once cast off all indecision and serve Christ, is a mere idle dream. It is the grace of the Spirit in our hearts, and not miracles, that our souls require. The Jews of our Lord's day are a standing proof to mankind that men may see signs and wonders, and yet remain hard as stone.

Expository Thoughts on John, 2.213
(also *Power and Sympathy of Christ,* 104-5).

A miracle would not be a miracle, if it could be explained!

Charges and Addresses, 238.

MONEY

A right use of our money in this world, from right motives, will be for our benefit in the world to come. It will not justify us. It will not bear the severity of God's judgment, any more than other good works. But it shall be an evidence of our grace, which shall befriend our souls. There is such a thing as 'laying up treasure in heaven,' and 'laying up a good foundation against the time to come' (Matt. 6:20; 1 Tim. 6:19).

Expository Thoughts on Luke, 2.152.

Money, in truth, is one of the most *unsatisfying* of possessions. It takes away some cares, no doubt; but it brings with it quite as many cares as it takes away. There is trouble in the getting of it. There is anxiety in the keeping of it. There are temptations in the use of it. There is guilt in the abuse of it. There is sorrow in the losing of it. There is perplexity in the disposing of it.

Practical Religion, 309.

Money is a good servant, but a bad master.

Practical Religion, 312.

Here we are for a few short years. How can we do most good with our money while we are here? How can we so spend it as to leave the world somewhat happier and somewhat holier when we are removed?

Practical Religion, 315-16.

Love of Money

Let us watch and pray against the love of money. It is a subtle disease, and often far nearer to us than we suppose. A poor man is just as liable to it as a rich man. It is possible to love money without having it, and it is possible to have it without loving it. Let us be 'content with such things as we have' (Heb. 13:5). We never know what we might do if we became suddenly rich. It is a striking fact, that there is only one prayer in all the book of Proverbs, and that one of the three petitions in that prayer, is the wise request,—'Give me neither poverty nor riches' (Prov. 30:8).

Expository Thoughts on Luke, 2.291.

MOSES

To the eye of sense there seemed no chance of their deliverance from Egyptian bondage, without a long and doubtful struggle. A settled home and country for them must have appeared a thing never likely to be obtained, however much desired. In fact, if ever man seemed to be choosing pain, trials, poverty, want, distress, anxiety, perhaps even death, with his eyes open, Moses was that man.

Holiness, 186.

Faith told him that there was a reward in heaven for the believer far richer than the treasures in Egypt, durable riches, where rust could not corrupt, nor thieves break through and steal. The crown there would be incorruptible; the weight of glory would be exceeding and eternal;—and faith bade him look away to an unseen heaven if his eyes were dazzled with Egyptian gold.

Holiness, 190.

MYSTERY

Things above our reason we must expect to find in Christianity.

Expository Thoughts on Luke, 2.380.

NEUTRALITY

We are always doing either good or harm.

Expository Thoughts on Luke, 2.88.

OBEDIENCE

Let us serve him faithfully as our Master. Let us obey him loyally as our King. Let us study his teaching as our Prophet. Let us walk diligently after him as our Example. Let us look anxiously for him as our coming Redeemer of body as well as soul. But above all, let us prize him as our Sacrifice, and rest our whole weight on his death as an atonement for sin.

Expository Thoughts on John, 1.40.

What he bids us do, he will give us grace to perform.

Expository Thoughts on John, 1.286.

A single day in hell will be worse than a whole life spent in carrying the cross.

Holiness, 108.

Every professing Christian is the soldier of Christ. He is bound by his baptism to fight Christ's battle against sin, the world, and the devil. The man that does not do this breaks his vow.

Holiness, 313.

Religious talking and profession are utterly worthless, without religious doing and practice.

Expository Thoughts on Luke, 1.70.

No man was ever sorry that he served the Lord. No man ever said at the end of his days, 'I have read my Bible too much, I have thought of God too much, I have prayed too much, I have been too careful about my soul.'

Old Paths, 399.

If friends will not walk in the narrow way with us, we must not walk in the broad way to please them.

Practical Religion, 283.

No one ever said at the end of his course that he had been too holy, and lived too near to God.

Practical Religion, 289.

If Christians were allowed to choose their own course through life, they would never learn hundreds of lessons about Christ and his grace, which they are now taught in God's ways. Let us remember these things. The time may come when we shall be called to take some journey in life which we greatly dislike. When that time comes, let us set out cheerfully, and believe that all is right.

Expository Thoughts on John, 2.178
(also *Power and Sympathy of Christ,* 27).

Let us do something worthy of our cause. The cause for which Jesus left heaven and came down to earth deserves the best that we can do.

Upper Room, 149.

OLD TESTAMENT

We must beware in these latter days of despising the Old Testament. It is one by-path to infidelity.

Expository Thoughts on John, 1.59.

Let it be a rule with us, in the reading of our Bibles, to study the types and ordinances of the Mosaic law with prayerful attention. They are all full of Christ. The altar, the scapegoat, the daily burnt-offering, the day of atonement, are all so many finger-posts pointing to the great sacrifice offered by our Lord on Calvary. Those who neglect to study the Jewish ordinances, as dark, dull, and uninteresting parts of the Bible, only show their own ignorance, and miss great advantages. Those who examine them with Christ as the key to their meaning, will find them full of gospel light and comfortable truth.

Expository Thoughts on Mark, 240-41.

We should always read the Old Testament with a desire to find something in it about Jesus Christ. We study this portion of the Bible with little profit, if we can see in it nothing but Moses, and David, and Samuel, and the prophets. Let us search the books of the Old Testament more closely. It was said by him whose words can never pass away, 'These are they which testify of me' (John 5:40).

Expository Thoughts on Mark, 2.

ORDINATION

I doubt the wisdom of the frequent proposals to extend and enlarge the diaconate, and to confer holy orders on a lower order of men. The plan, if adopted, would lower the standard of ministerial qualifications. To this I am entirely opposed. I speak after the experience of nine years' ordinations, and I say that the standard is quite low enough already.

Charges and Addresses, 222.

PATIENCE

I would rather tolerate much chaff in the church than cast out one grain of wheat.

Practical Religion, 420.

PEACE

'Peace' and not blame,—'peace' and not fault-finding,—'peace' and not rebuke,—was the first word which this little company heard from their Master's lips, after he left the tomb.

Expository Thoughts on John, 3.282.

Let it be noted, that 'peace' was the last word in the prophetical hymn of Zacharias,—'peace on earth,' part of the good news proclaimed by angels when Christ was born,—'peace' the proclamation which the seventy disciples were ordered to make in every house which they visited,—'peace' the legacy which our Lord left and gave to the apostles on the night before he was crucified,—and 'peace' was the first word which he spoke when he appeared among them again after his resurrection (Luke 1:79; 2:14; 10:5; John 14:27).

Expository Thoughts on Luke, 2.381-82.

When hunger can be relieved without food, and thirst quenched without drink, and weariness removed without rest, then, and not till then, will men find peace without Christ.

Old Paths, 212.

Governments cannot give it. Education will not impart it. Worldly amusements cannot supply it. Money will not purchase it. It can only be found in the hand of Jesus Christ, and to his hand you must turn, if you would find peace within.

Christmas Thoughts, 23.

PERFECTIONISM

Do not suppose the day will ever come when you will find no weak point in your heart, no wanderings in private prayer, no distraction in Bible-reading, no cold desires in the public worship of God, no flesh to mortify, no devil to tempt, no worldly snares to make you fall. Expect nothing of the kind. Conversion is not perfection! Conversion is not heaven! The old man within you is yet alive; the world around you is yet full of danger; the devil is not dead. Remember at your best, that a converted sinner is still a poor weak sinner, needing Christ every day. Remember this, and you will not be disappointed.

Old Paths, 318.

Absolute perfection is for heaven, and not for earth, where we have a weak body, a wicked world, and a busy devil continually near our souls.

Practical Religion, 11.

PERSECUTION

Has the true church been oppressed in one country? It has fled to another.—Has it been trampled on and oppressed in one soil? It has taken root and flourished in some other climate.—Fire, sword, prisons, fines, penalties, have never been able to destroy its vitality. Its persecutors have died and gone to their own place, but the Word of God has lived, and grown, and multiplied. Weak as this true church may appear to the eye of man, it is an anvil which has broken many a hammer in times past, and perhaps will break many more before the end.

Holiness, 297-98.

Not all the power of Satan can cast out of Christ's true church one single believer.

Holiness, 299.

Thousands have been burned, or shot, or hanged, or drowned, or beheaded, in the name of the gospel, and those who have slain them have actually believed that they were doing God service! Unhappily, they have only shown their own ignorance of the spirit of the gospel, and the mind of Christ.

Expository Thoughts on Luke, 1.255.

Encouragement in Persecution

The blood that his saints have shed in his name will all be reckoned for one day. The tears that often flow so freely in consequence of the unkindness of the wicked, will one day be wiped from all faces. And when … all who have suffered for the truth are at last gathered together, they will find it true that heaven makes amends for all.

Expository Thoughts on Luke, 1.76

PERSEVERANCE OF THE SAINTS

They never perish, because he never ceases to pray for them, and his prayer must prevail.

Expository Thoughts on John, 3.137.

Multitudes are every year turning out of the broad way and entering the narrow. None who really enter the narrow way grow tired of it and return to the broad. The footsteps in the downward road are often to be seen turning out of it. The footsteps in the road to heaven are all one way.

Holiness, 108.

It is no easy matter for a man to carry the cross and reach heaven.

Old Paths, 416.

When I speak of the doctrine of perseverance, I mean this. I say that the Bible teaches that true believers, real genuine Christians, shall persevere in their religion to the end of their lives. They shall never perish. They shall never be lost. They shall never be cast away. Once in Christ, they shall always be in Christ. Once made children of God by adoption and grace, they shall never cease to be his children and become children of the devil. Once endued with the grace of the

Spirit, that grace shall never be taken from them. Once pardoned and forgiven, they shall never be deprived of their pardon. Once joined to Christ by living faith, their union shall never be broken off. Once called by God into the narrow way that leads to life, they shall never be allowed to fall into hell.

Old Paths, 449.

They that persevere to the end are not dependent on any means, but still they are not independent of them. Their final salvation does not hang on their obedience to practical exhortations, but it is just in taking heed to such exhortations that they will always continue to the end. It is the diligent, the watchful, the prayerful, and the humble, to whom belongs the promise,—'They shall never perish.'

Old Paths, 454.

Once admit that the saints of God may perish, and you seem to me to tear from the gospel crown its brightest jewel. We are hanging on the edge of a precipice. We are kept in awful suspense until we are dead. To tell us that there are plenty of gracious promises to encourage us, if we will only persevere, is but mockery. It is like telling the sick man that if he will only get well he will be strong.

Old Paths, 474.

Let any thinking man look at the two ways in which the weary and heavy-laden sinner may be addressed, and judge for himself which is most like the gospel of the grace of God. On the one side stands the doctrine, which says, 'Believe on the Lord Jesus Christ and thou shalt be saved. Once believing thou shalt never perish. Thy faith shall never be allowed entirely to fail. Thou shalt be sealed by the Holy Spirit unto the day of redemption'. On the other side stands the doctrine, which says, 'Believe on the Lord Jesus Christ and thou shalt be saved. But after thou hast believed take care. Thy faith may fail. Thou mayest fall away. Thou mayest drive the Spirit from thee. Thou mayest at length perish everlastingly.'—Which doctrine of these two contains most good news?

Old Paths, 475.

Can you think he would suffer on the cross and die, and yet leave it uncertain whether believers in him would be saved? Can you think he would wrestle with death and hell, and go down to the grave for our sakes, and yet allow our eternal life to hang on such a thread as our poor miserable endeavours?

Practical Religion, 428.

The members of God's family shall all be *brought safe home* one day. Here upon earth they may be scattered, tried, tossed with tempests, and bowed down with afflictions. But not one of them shall perish (John 10:28).

Christmas Thoughts, 68.

Perseverance unto Death

Doctors may have given over their labours; friends may be unable to minister to thy wants; sight may depart; hearing may depart; memory may be almost gone: but the lovingkindness of God shall not depart. Once in Christ thou shalt never be forsaken. Jesus shall stand by thee. Satan shall not harm thee. Death shall not separate thee from the everlasting love of God in Christ. Thou shalt never perish.

Old Paths, 484.

PETER, APOSTLE

Peter, we may be sure, did far less good when he drew his sword and cut off a man's ear, than he did when he stood calmly before the council as a prisoner, and said, 'We cannot but speak the things which we have seen and heard' (Acts 4:20).

Expository Thoughts on Luke, 2.321.

Once we find him trying to keep back our Lord, as far as he could, from the great work of the cross, and severely rebuked. Then we find him denying the Lord three times, and with an oath.

Knots Untied, 407.

Let the meekness of St Peter in taking a reproof, be as much our example as the boldness of St Paul in reproving. Happy is the Christian who can call the person who rebukes him faithfully, a 'beloved brother' (2 Pet. 3:15).

Knots Untied, 428.

PHARISEES AND SADDUCEES

Party spirit was most bitter and intense, notwithstanding a thin mask of external unity: the Pharisees hated the Sadducees and the Sadducees the Pharisees, and neither party would have any dealings with the Samaritans. Worst of all, with the Old Testament in their hands and the clearest evidence under their eyes, they would not believe that Jesus was the promised Messiah.

Charges and Addresses, 200-1.

The doctrine of the Pharisees may be summed up in three words,—they were formalists, tradition-worshippers, and self-righteous.

Knots Untied, 367.

He [Jesus] knew that their succession would never fail, and their generation never become extinct,—and that though the names of

Pharisees and Sadducees were no more, yet their principles would always exist. He knew that during the time that the church existed, until his return, there would always be some that would add to the word, and some that would subtract from it,—some that would stifle it, by adding to it other things, and some that would bleed it to death, by subtracting from its principal truths. And this is the reason why we find him delivering this solemn warning: 'Take heed and beware of the leaven of the Pharisees and of the Sadducees.'

Knots Untied, 369.

PHILOSOPHY

It is poor philosophy to say we will believe nothing unless we can understand everything!

Is All Scripture Inspired? 3.

When St Paul quoted lines from heathen poets he did not mean us to regard them as inspired. But he was taught by God to clothe his ideas in the words which they had used, and by so doing he very likely obtained a favourable reading from many.

Old Paths, 26.

The simple questions, 'What is life, and what is death?' contain enough to silence the wisest philosopher.

Expository Thoughts on John, 2.193
(also *Power and Sympathy of Christ,* 59).

A follower of Socrates or Plato might have talked well and eloquently on many subjects, but he could have never answered the jailor's question, 'What must I do to be saved?' (Acts 16:30). He could never have said in his last hour, 'O death, where is thy sting? O grave, where is thy victory?'

Upper Room, 134.

POLITICS

That which is morally wrong can never be politically right. To govern only for the sake of pleasing and benefiting the majority, without any reference to the eternal principles of justice, right, and mercy, may be *expedient* and please man; but it does not please God.

Expository Thoughts on John, 2.219
(also *Power and Sympathy of Christ,* 116).

Does a State want its subjects to be provident, truthful, diligent, temperate, honest, moral, and charitable? Does it or does it not? If it does it ought to encourage, and not to ignore, religion. To punish vice and yet not cherish virtue, to spend public money on building jails and yet not encourage Christianity, is, to say the least, an absurdly inconsistent policy. The more true religion the better subjects! The more good subjects the more prosperity!

Charges and Addresses, 325.

Political Leaders

It is easy to criticise and find fault with their conduct and write furious articles against them in newspapers, or make violent speeches about them on platforms. Any fool can rip and rend a costly garment, but not every man can cut out and make one. To expect perfection in kings, prime ministers, or rulers of any kind, is senseless and unreasonable. We should exhibit more wisdom if we prayed for them more, and criticised less.

Upper Room, 401.

POOR

Let us beware of despising the poor, because of their poverty. Their condition is one which the Son of God has sanctified and honoured, by taking it voluntarily on himself. God is no respecter of persons. He looks at the hearts of men, and not at their incomes. Let us never be ashamed of the cross of poverty, if God thinks fit to lay it upon us. To be godless and covetous is disgraceful, but it is no disgrace to be poor. A mean dwelling place, and coarse food, and a hard bed, are not pleasing to flesh and blood. But they are the portion which the Lord Jesus himself willingly accepted from the day of his entrance into the world. Wealth ruins far more souls than poverty. When the love of money begins to creep over us, let us think of the manger at Bethlehem, and of him who was laid in it. Such thoughts may deliver us from much harm.

Expository Thoughts on Luke, 1.41.

Settle it in your mind that the main cause of all the suffering you see around you is sin. Sin is the grand cause of the enormous luxury of the rich, and the painful degradation of the poor,—of the heartless selfishness of the highest classes, and the helpless poverty of the lowest. Sin must be first cast out of the world. The hearts of all men must be renewed and sanctified. The devil must be bound. The Prince of Peace must come down and take his great power and reign. All this must be before there ever can be universal happiness, or the gulf be filled up which now divides the rich and poor.

Practical Religion, 298.

The words 'rich' and 'poor' will change their meaning entirely one day. He is the only rich man who has come to Christ by faith, and from Christ has received rest.

Christmas Thoughts, 21.

PRAYER

The Lord Jesus is far more ready to hear than we are to pray, and far more ready to give favours than we are to ask them.

Expository Thoughts on John, 1.143.

And it is a curious fact … that many who profess to deny man's impotence in theory often confess it in their prayers and praises, almost in spite of themselves. Many people are very low Arminians in print or in the pulpit, but excellent Calvinists on their knees.

Expository Thoughts on John, 1.271.

The confessional we want is not a box in the vestry, but the throne of grace.

Holiness, 409.

We are taught to approach him as our Father in heaven,—our Father no doubt as our Creator, but specially as our Father reconciled to us in Christ Jesus,—our Father whose dwelling is 'in heaven,' and whom no temple on earth can contain.

Expository Thoughts on Luke, 2.1-2.

A prayer which only contains thanksgiving and profession, and asks nothing, is essentially defective. It may be suitable for an angel, but it is not suitable for a sinner.

Expository Thoughts on Luke, 2.194.

Prayer is the most important subject in practical religion.

Practical Religion, 59.

We cannot know God in Christ, unless we speak to him in prayer. If we wish to be with him in heaven, we must be his friends on earth. If we wish to be his friends on earth, *we must pray*.

Practical Religion, 60.

I have read the lives of many eminent Christians who have been on earth since the Bible days. Some of them, I see, were rich, and some poor. Some were learned, and some unlearned. Some of them were Episcopalians, some Presbyterians, some Baptists, some Independents. Some were Calvinists, and some Arminians. Some have loved to use a liturgy, and some to use none. But one thing, I see, they all had in common. They have all been *men of prayer*.

Practical Religion, 62.

Prayer opened the Red Sea. Prayer brought water from the rock and bread from heaven. Prayer made the sun stand still. Prayer brought fire from the sky on Elijah's sacrifice. Prayer turned the counsel of Ahithophel into foolishness. Prayer overthrew the army of Sennacherib. Well might Mary, Queen of Scots, say, 'I fear John Knox's prayers more than an army of ten thousand men.'

Practical Religion, 68-69.

When Abraham spoke to God, he said, 'I am dust and ashes.' When Job spoke, he said, 'I am vile' (Gen. 18:27; Job 40:4). Let us do likewise.

Practical Religion, 81.

Never think that time is wasted which is given to God.

Practical Religion, 83.

Let us settle it down in our minds, that cold prayers are a sacrifice without fire.

Practical Religion, 83.

Faith is to prayer what the feather is to the arrow: without it prayer will not hit the mark.

Practical Religion, 84.

Think of Daniel. He had all the business of a kingdom on his hands; yet he prayed three times a day. See there the secret of his safety in wicked Babylon.

Thoughts for Young Men, 70.

Prayer is the very life-breath of true religion. It is one of the first evidences that a man is born again. 'Behold,' said the Lord of Saul, in the day he sent Ananias to him, 'Behold, he prayeth' (Acts 9:11).

Upper Room, 252.

Above all, water all your work with prayer for the blessing of the Holy Ghost, and let your path to the throne of grace be never overgrown with weeds.

Charges and Addresses, 282.

A young Christian once said to an old one, 'My prayers are so poor and weak, that I cannot think they are of any use.' The old Christian replied, with deep wisdom, 'Only place them in Christ's hands, and he makes them look so different in heaven that you would hardly know them again.'

Knots Untied, 279.

Praying for Children

Great is the power of prayer and intercession! The child of many prayers shall seldom be cast away. God's time of conversion may not be ours. He may think fit to prove our faith by keeping us long waiting. But so long as a child lives, and a parent prays, we have no right to despair about that child's soul.

Expository Thoughts on Luke, 1.246.

Praying to Saints

There is *no warrant of Scripture* for such a confession. There is not a text in the Bible that bids us confess to dead saints and angels. There is not an instance in Scripture of any living believer taking his sins to them.

Knots Untied, 300.

Prayerlessness

Praying and sinning will never live together in the same heart. Prayer will consume sin, or sin will choke prayer.

Practical Religion, 66.

PREACHING

If there is no salvation excepting by Christ, we must not be surprised if ministers of the gospel preach much about him. They cannot tell us too much about the name which is above every name. We cannot hear of him too often. We may hear too much about controversy in sermons,—we may hear too much of works and duties, of forms, of ceremonies, of sacraments and ordinances,—but there is one subject which we never hear too much of: we can never hear too much of Christ.

Knots Untied, 47-48.

A morbid dislike to strong language,—an excessive fear of giving offence,—a constant flinching from directness and plain speaking, are, unhappily, too much the characteristics of the modern Christian pulpit.

Expository Thoughts on Luke, 1.69.

Let us beware of despising preaching. In every age of the church, it has been God's principal instrument for the awakening of sinners and the edifying of saints. The days when there has been little or no preaching have been days when there has been little or no good done in the church.

Expository Thoughts on Luke, 1.99

Faithful ministers should always denounce sin most plainly, when their churches are most full, and their congregations most large. Then is the time to 'cry aloud and spare not,' and show people their sins. It is a snare to some ministers, to flatter full congregations and scold thin ones. Such dealing is very unlike that of our Lord.

Expository Thoughts on Luke, 1.194.

It is, in fact, God's chosen instrument for doing good to souls. By it sinners are converted, inquirers led on, and saints built up. A preaching ministry is absolutely essential to the health and prosperity of a visible church. The pulpit is the place where the chief victories of the gospel have always been won, and no church has ever done much for the advancement of true religion in which the pulpit has been neglected. Would we know whether a minister is a truly apostolical man? If he is, he will give the best of his attention to his sermons.

Expository Thoughts on Luke, 1.223.

'He speaks the best who turns the ear into an eye.'

Practical Religion, 296.

We would realize the character given by Charles II of one of his preachers: 'That man preaches as though death was behind his back. When I hear him I cannot go to sleep.'

Practical Religion, 304.

To attain simplicity in preaching is *of the utmost importance* to every minister who wishes to be useful to souls.

Simplicity in Preaching, 4.

Mind, then, when your text is chosen, that you understand it and see right through it; that you know precisely what you want to prove, what you want to teach, what you want to establish, and what you want people's minds to carry away. If you yourself begin in a fog, you may depend upon it you will leave your people in darkness. Cicero, one of the greatest ancient orators, said long ago,— 'No one can possibly speak clearly and eloquently about a subject which he does not understand,'—and I am satisfied that he spoke the truth.

Simplicity in Preaching, 7.

I am not a bit ashamed to say that I often read the sermons of Mr Spurgeon.

Simplicity in Preaching, 10.

We should bear in mind that preachers have to do with hearers and not readers, and that what will 'read' well will not always 'speak' well. A reader of English can always help himself by looking back a few lines and refreshing his mind. A hearer of English hears once for all, and if he loses the thread of your sermon in a long involved sentence, he very likely never finds it again.

Simplicity in Preaching, 13.

If Christ crucified has not his rightful place in your sermons, and sin is not exposed as it should be, and your people are not plainly told what they ought to believe, and be, and do, *your preaching is of no use*.

Simplicity in Preaching, 21.

You must speak *from* the heart if you wish to speak *to* the heart, and that there must be unmistakable faith and conviction within the pulpit if there is to be faith and conviction among the pews.

Christian Leaders of the Eighteenth Century, 15.

(1.) Preach Christ crucified, and dwell chiefly on the blessings resulting from his righteousness, atonement, and intercession. (2.) Avoid all needless controversies in the pulpit; except it be when your subject necessarily requires it, or when the truths of God are likely to suffer by your silence. (3.) When you ascend the pulpit, leave your learning behind you: endeavour to preach more to the hearts of your people than to their heads. (4.) Do not affect much oratory. Seek rather to profit than to be admired.

Christian Leaders of the Eighteenth Century, 352.

Let your sermons be addresses in which Christ's blood, mediation, and intercession; Christ's love, power, and willingness to save; the real work of the Holy Ghost, repentance, faith, and holiness; are never wanting—sermons full of life, and fire, and power; sermons which set hearers thinking, and make them go home to pray.

Charges and Addresses, 107.

Aims of Preaching

Are their hearts and consciences better? Is sin more hateful? Is Christ more precious? Is holiness more desired? Are they becoming more ready for death, judgment, and eternity every week that they live? These are the grand ends which every clergyman should set before him in every service which he conducts.

Charges and Addresses, 108.

Hearing the Word Preached

Preaching is an ordinance of which the value can never be overrated in the church of Christ. But it should never be forgotten, that there must not only be good preaching, but good hearing.

Expository Thoughts on Luke, 1.191.

Would anyone know how to hear aright? Then let him lay to heart three simple rules. For one thing, we must hear with faith, believing implicitly that every word of God is true, and shall stand. The word in old time did not profit the Jews, 'not being mixed with faith in them that heard it' (Heb. 4:2).—For another thing, we must hear with reverence, remembering constantly that the Bible is the book of God. This was the habit of the Thessalonians. They received Paul's message, 'not as the word of men, but the word of God' (1 Thess. 2:13).—Above all, we must hear with prayer, praying for God's blessing before the sermon is preached, praying for God's blessing again when the sermon is over. Here lies the grand defect of the hearing of many. They ask no blessing, and so they have none.

Expository Thoughts on Luke, 1.197.

Powerless Preaching

The popular sermon in this day is far too often a mere exhibition of intellectual fireworks, very pleasant to the many hearers who only like temporary excitement, and dislike any preaching which pricks their consciences and makes them uncomfortable, but utterly destitute of distinct doctrine; and powerless to move hearts or affect lives.

Charges and Addresses, 226.

Incessant running after sensational preachers; incessant attendance at hot, crowded meetings protracted to late hours; incessant craving after fresh excitement and highly-spiced pulpit novelties—all this kind of thing is calculated to produce a very unhealthy style of

Christianity; and, in many cases, I am afraid, the end is utter ruin of soul.

Charges and Addresses, 250.

Preaching Christ, Its Necessity

Christ is the grand subject which every faithful minister exalts in the pulpit. Christ is the object that every true pastor sets before dying people on their deathbeds. Christ is the great source of light and peace and hope. There is not a spark of spiritual comfort that has ever illumined a sinner's heart, that has not come from Christ.

Christmas Thoughts, 37.

We must make 'Christ crucified and risen again' the sun and centre of our sermons.

Charges and Addresses, 205.

The sermon full of Christ is the sermon which the Holy Spirit most usually blesses to the souls of all classes.

Charges and Addresses, 205.

Sermon Delivery

Every sensible Christian knows well that voice and delivery have a great deal to say to the effectiveness of a speaker, and above all of one who speaks in the pulpit. A sermon faultless both in doctrine and composition will often sound dull and tiresome, when tamely read by a clergyman with a heavy monotonous manner.

Christian Leaders of the Eighteenth Century, 185.

Sermon Illustrations

If you pause in your sermon, and say, 'Now I will tell you a story,' I engage that all who are not too fast asleep will prick up their ears and listen. People like similes, illustrations, and well-told stories, and will listen to them when they will attend to nothing else.

Simplicity in Preaching, 16.

PRIDE

So long as the world stands, Christ and his gospel will be a stumbling-block to many. To hear that we are all lost and guilty sinners, and cannot save ourselves,—to hear that we must give up our own righteousness, and trust in One who was crucified between two thieves,—to hear that we must be content to enter heaven side by side with publicans and harlots, and to owe all our salvation to free grace,—this is always offensive to the natural man. Our proud hearts do not like it. We are offended.

Expository Thoughts on Luke, 1.167.

It is a quaint and homely saying, but only too true, that no pope has ever received such honour as Pope 'Self.'

Expository Thoughts on Luke, 1.250.

Who does not know that pride, and haughtiness, and high-mindedness, and readiness to take offence, and implacable determination never to forget and never to forgive, are common among baptized men and women? Thousands will go to the Lord's table, and even profess to love the gospel, who fire up in a moment at the least appearance of what they call 'offensive' conduct, and make a quarrel out of the merest trifles.

Expository Thoughts on Luke, 2.166.

Pride, self-conceit, and a disposition to look down on others as ignorant, blind, and inferior to ourselves, are faults to which many converted people are peculiarly liable.

Expository Thoughts on Luke, 2.196.

Pride is the oldest sin in the world. Indeed, it was before the world. Satan and his angels fell by pride. They were not satisfied with their first estate. Thus, pride stocked hell with its first inhabitants.

Thoughts for Young Men, 19.

The older you grow, and the more you see, the less reason you will find for being proud.

Thoughts for Young Men, 21.

PROCRASTINATION

Tomorrow is the devil's day, but today is God's. Satan cares not how spiritual your intentions may be, and how holy your resolutions, if only they are fixed for *tomorrow*.

Thoughts for Young Men, 7.

The notice to quit this mortal body sometimes comes very suddenly, and men and women are summoned to go forth in a moment into the unseen world. You had better use time while you have it, and not make shipwreck on that miserable rock, 'a convenient season.'

Upper Room, 216.

PROPHECY

It was Christ of whom all the prophets from Isaiah to Malachi spoke. They saw through a glass darkly. They sometimes dwelt on his sufferings, and sometimes on his glory that should follow (1 Pet. 1:11). They did not always mark out for us the distinction between Christ's first coming and Christ's second coming. Like two candles in a straight line, one behind the other, they sometimes saw both the advents at the same time, and spoke of them in one breath. They were sometimes moved by the Holy Ghost to write of the times of Christ crucified, and sometimes of Christ's kingdom in the latter days. But Jesus dying, or Jesus reigning, was the thought you will ever find uppermost in their minds.

Holiness, 421-22.

PROVIDENCE

The overruling providence of God appears in this simple fact. He orders all things in heaven and earth. He turns the hearts of kings whithersoever he will. He overruled the time when Augustus decreed the taxing. He directed the enforcement of the decree in such a way, that Mary must needs be at Bethlehem when 'the days were accomplished that she should be delivered.' Little did the haughty Roman emperor, and his officer Cyrenius, think that they were only instruments in the hand of the God of Israel, and were only carrying out the eternal purposes of the King of kings. Little did they think that they were helping to lay the foundation of a kingdom, before which the empires of this world would all go down one day, and Roman idolatry pass away.

Expository Thoughts on Luke, 1.39-40.

We are like children who look at a half-finished building, and have not the least idea what it will look like when it is completed. They see masses of stone, and brick, and rubbish, and timber, and mortar, and scaffolding, and dirt, and all in apparent confusion. But the architect who designed the building sees order in all, and quietly looks forward with joy to the day when the whole building will be finished, and the scaffolding removed and taken away. It is even so with us. We cannot grasp the meaning of many a providence in our lives, and are tempted to think that all around us is confusion.

But we should try to remember that the great Architect in heaven is always doing wisely and well, and that we are always being 'led by the right way to a city of habitation' (Psa. 107:7). The resurrection morning will explain all.

Upper Room, 224.

PSALMS

We have probably little idea how much deep truth is contained in the book of Psalms. No part of the Bible perhaps is better known in the letter, and none so little understood in the spirit. We err greatly if we suppose that it is nothing but a record of David's feelings, of David's experience, David's praises, and David's prayers. The hand that held the pen was generally David's. But the subject matter was often something far deeper and higher than the history of the son of Jesse. The book of Psalms, in a word, is a book full of Christ,—Christ suffering,—Christ in humiliation,—Christ dying,—Christ rising again,—Christ coming the second time,—Christ reigning over all. Both the advents are here,—the advent in suffering to bear the cross,—the advent in power to wear the crown. Both the kingdoms are here,—the kingdom of grace, during which the elect are gathered,—the kingdom of glory, when every tongue shall confess that Jesus is Lord. Let us always read the Psalms with a peculiar reverence. Let us say to ourselves as we read, 'A greater than David is here.'

Expository Thoughts on Luke, 2.257.

PURGATORY

There is no such thing as purgatory, whatever some Christians may think fit to say. There is no house of training or probation for those who are not true Christians when they die.

Christmas Thoughts, 61.

REDEMPTION

No gold, no silver, no diamonds were found sufficient to provide redemption: no angel in heaven was able to bring a ransom. Nothing but the blood of Christ,—nothing but the death of the eternal Son of God upon the cross, was found sufficient to buy for the soul deliverance from hell.

Old Paths, 50.

He laid down his life to pay the price of our redemption: he died that we might live; he suffered that we might reign; he bore shame that we might receive glory.

Practical Religion, 320.

REFORMATION, THE

To the Reformation Englishmen owe an English Bible, and liberty for every man to read it. To the Reformation they owe the knowledge of the way of peace with God, and of the right of every sinner to go straight to Christ by faith, without bishop, priest, or minister standing in his way.

Light from Old Times, 68-69.

When a man makes an idol of Fathers and councils, and disparages the theology of the Reformation, we may be sure there is a screw loose in his theology.

Light from Old Times, 230-31.

The Reformers

They had to take down an old decayed house, and re-build it from the very ground. It is nonsense to criticise their proceedings, as if they voyaged over a smooth sea, with a fair wind, and a clear course. On the contrary, they had to pilot the ship of true religion through a narrow and difficult strait, against current, wind, and tide. Put all their difficulties together, the arbitrary, profligate character of Henry VIII, and the tender years of Edward VI, the general ignorance of the population, the bitter enmity of dispossessed monks and friars, the open opposition of many of the bishops, and the secret indifference of a vast proportion of the clergy,—put all these things together, and weigh them well; and then I think you will not lightly regard the work that the early Reformers did. For my own part, so far from wondering that they did so little, I wonder rather that they did so much.

Light from Old Times, 129.

REGRET

Sin is the mother of all sorrow, and no sort of sin appears to give a man so much misery and pain as the sins of his youth. The foolish acts he did,—the time he wasted,—the mistakes he made,—the bad company he kept,—the harm he did himself, both body and soul,—the chances of happiness he threw away,—the openings of usefulness he neglected; —all these are things that often embitter the conscience of an old man, throw a gloom on the evening of his days, and fill the later hours of his life with self-reproach and shame.

Thoughts for Young Men, 14-15.

Old wounds will often ache and give pain long after they are healed, and only a scar remains:—so may you find it with your sins.

Thoughts for Young Men, 17.

RELIGION

Surely to be satisfied with a religion which neither gives peace in life, nor hope in death, nor glory in the world to come, is childish folly.

Old Paths, 66.

We want you to understand that religion does not consist in professing certain opinions, and performing certain outward duties, and going through certain outward forms. It consists in being reconciled to God, and enjoying peace with him. It consists in having our sins cleansed away, and knowing that they are cleansed. It consists in being brought back into friendship with the King of kings, and living in the sunshine of that friendship.

Old Paths, 150.

True religion must never expect to be popular.

Practical Religion, 257.

REPENTANCE

We must carefully bear in mind, that no repentance can make atonement for sin. The blood of Christ, and nothing else, can wash away sin from man's soul. No quantity of repentance can ever justify us in the sight of God. 'We are accounted righteous before God, only for the sake of our Lord Jesus Christ, by faith, and not for our own works or deservings.' It is of the utmost importance to understand this clearly. The trouble that men bring upon their souls, by misunderstanding this subject, is more than can be expressed.

But while we say all this, we must carefully remember that without repentance no soul was ever yet saved. We must know our sins, mourn over them, forsake them, abhor them, or else we shall never enter the kingdom of heaven. There is nothing meritorious in this. It forms no part whatever of the price of our redemption. Our salvation is all of grace, from first to last.

Expository Thoughts on Luke, 1.67.

The nature of true repentance is clearly and unmistakably laid down in Holy Scripture. It begins with knowledge of sin. It goes on to work sorrow for sin. It leads to confession of sin before God. It shows itself before man by a thorough breaking off from sin. It results in producing a habit of deep hatred for all sin. Above all, it is inseparably connected with lively faith in the Lord Jesus Christ. Repentance like this is the characteristic of all true Christians.

Expository Thoughts on Luke, 2.82.

Here lies the grand distinction between 'repentance unto salvation,' and unavailing remorse. Remorse can make a man miserable, like Judas Iscariot, but it can do no more. It does not lead him to God.—Repentance makes a man's heart soft and his conscience tender, and shows itself in real turning to a Father in heaven. The falls of a graceless professor are falls from which there is no rising again. But the fall of a true saint always ends in deep contrition, self-abasement, and amendment of life.

Expository Thoughts on Luke, 2.327.

People generally die just as they have lived. True repentance is never too late:—but repentance deferred to the last hours of life is seldom true.

Old Paths, 79.

The tears of repentance wash away no sins. It is bad divinity to say that they do.

Old Paths, 386.

You think us extreme when we beseech you to repent and be converted. You think we ask too much when we urge you to come out from the world, and take up the cross, and follow Christ. But take notice that you will one day confess that *we were right.* Sooner or later, in this world or the next, you will acknowledge that you were wrong.

Practical Religion, 37.

Repentance and faith are the gifts of God, and gifts that he often withholds, when they have been long offered in vain. I grant you true repentance is never too late, but I warn you at the same time, late repentance is seldom true.

Thoughts for Young Men, 10.

REPROBATION

There is no such a thing as decreed damnation in the Bible. The offers of the gospel are wide, free, and general. 'In all our doings,' says the 17th Article, 'that will of God is to be followed, which we have expressly declared to us in the word of God.' God's sovereignty was never meant to destroy man's responsibility. One thief was saved that no sinner might despair, but only one, that no sinner might presume.

Expository Thoughts on Luke, 2.350.

REST

Come to me, says the world, and I will give you riches and pleasure. Come with me, says the devil, and I will give you greatness, power, and wisdom. 'Come unto me,' says the Lord Jesus Christ, 'and I will give you rest.'

Christmas Thoughts, 16.

RESURRECTION

The grave itself is a conquered enemy. It must render back its tenants safe and sound, the very moment that Christ calls for them at the last day.

Let us remember these things when those whom we love fall asleep in Christ, or when we ourselves receive our notice to depart this world.

Expository Thoughts on John, 2.179
(also *Power and Sympathy of Christ,* 28).

RETALIATION

To give blow for blow, and violence for violence, anger for anger, and abuse for abuse, is the conduct of a dog or a heathen, but not of a Christian.

Expository Thoughts on Luke, 1.144.

REWARDS

The wages which Christ will give to his believing people will be far out of proportion to anything they have done for him. Their tears will be found in his bottle. Their least desires to do good will be found recorded. Their weakest efforts to glorify him will be found written in his book of remembrance. Not a cup of cold water shall miss its reward.

Expository Thoughts on Luke, 2.303.

ROMAN CATHOLICISM

We may safely affirm that none would be more forward to reprove the honour paid by the Romish Church to the Virgin Mary, than the Virgin Mary herself.

Expository Thoughts on Luke, 1.27.

No people can be more zealous than the Romish priests in honouring the tombs and relics of saints and martyrs, and building costly churches in honour of them. And yet the doctrines of these saints are not believed, and their are lives are not imitated!

Expository Thoughts on Luke, 2.41.

What is the essence of Romanism, and semi-Romanism, and formalism, and sacrament-worship and church-adorning, and ceremonialism? What is it all but the leaven of the Pharisees under one shape or another? The Pharisees are not extinct. Pharisaism lives still.

Expository Thoughts on Luke, 2.44.

To talk of the Virgin Mary as being more compassionate than Christ is a proof of miserable ignorance. To flee to the saints for comfort, when we may flee to Christ, is an act of mingled stupidity and blasphemy, and a robbery of Christ's crown.

Expository Thoughts on Luke, 2.390.

The Christian minister is a teacher, an ambassador, a messenger, a watchman, a witness, a shepherd, a steward, and is expressly authorized by the Epistles to Timothy and Titus, where his duties are clearly laid down. But there is a conspicuous absence of New Testament proof that he is a sacrificing priest.

Upper Room, 280.

If the recent decree of Rome had formally announced to the world that the Pope admits the validity of our orders, and recognizes all Anglican clergymen as Catholic priests, it would not make a jot of difference to me. It is doctrine, doctrine, and not orders, which makes the insuperable objection to reunion with Rome.

Charges and Addresses, 372.

She sends men to priests and confessors, to penance and absolution, to masses and extreme unction, to fasting and bodily mortification, to the Virgin Mary and the saints,—as if these things could add to the safety there is in Christ Jesus. And in doing this she sins against the doctrine of God's word with a high hand.

Knots Untied, 41.

No Romish teacher, if he is faithful to his Church, can say to an anxious sinner, 'Believe on the Lord Jesus Christ and thou shalt be saved.' He cannot do it without additions and explanations, which completely destroy the good news. He dare not give the gospel medicine, without adding something which destroys its efficacy, and neutralizes its power. Purgatory, penance, priestly absolution, the intercession of saints, the worship of the virgin, and many other man-made services of popery, all spring from this source. They are all rotten props to support weary consciences. But they are rendered necessary by the denial of justification by faith.

Knots Untied, 423.

ROMAINE, WILLIAM

The Rector of St George's, who first invited Romaine to take the office, and then at the end of five years removed him from it, was Dr Andrew Trebeck. His appointment was owing to his high character and reputation, and not to personal friendship; his removal was caused by the popularity and plainness of his ministry. The real truth was, that his preaching attracted such crowds to the old parish church, that the regular seat-holders took offence, and complained that they were put to inconvenience. Strong pressure was brought to bear upon the rector; and he, 'willing to please' the parishioners, gave Romaine notice to terminate his engagement. This notice he received quietly, saying, that 'he was willing to relinquish the office, hoping that his doctrine had been Christian, and owning the inconvenience which had attended the parishioners'. A more discreditable affair than this probably never disfigured the parochial annals of the diocese of London. An eminent and godly clergyman was removed from his post because he attracted too many hearers! And yet, at this very time, scores of clergymen in London churches were no doubt preaching every week to empty benches or to congregations of half-a-dozen people, without anyone interfering with them!

Christian Leaders of the Eighteenth Century, 144-45.

He stood in the same place, constantly preaching to the same hearers, and not able, like Whitefield, Wesley, Grimshaw, and other itinerant brethren, to preach old sermons. He stood there witnessing to truths which were most unpopular, and brought down on him opposition, persecution, and scorn. He stood in a most public post, continually watched, observed, and noticed by unfriendly eyes, ready to detect faults in a moment if he committed them.

Christian Leaders of the Eighteenth Century, 163.

ROWLAND, DANIEL

When a backslider was pointed out to him, who had once been one of his followers, he said: 'It is to be feared indeed that he is one of *my* disciples; for had he been one of *my Lord's* disciples, he would not have been in such a state of sin and rebellion.'

Christian Leaders of the Eighteenth Century, 195.

He often used to say, during his latter days, that there were four lessons which he had laboured to learn throughout the whole course of his religious life, and yet that he was but a dull scholar even in his old age. These lessons were the following—(1) To repent without despairing; (2) To believe without being presumptuous; (3) To rejoice without falling into levity; (4) To be angry without sinning.

Christian Leaders of the Eighteenth Century, 195.

SABBATH

Let us never forget that our feelings about Sundays are sure tests of the state of our souls. The man who can find no pleasure in giving God one day in the week, is manifestly unfit for heaven. Heaven itself is nothing but an eternal sabbath. If we cannot enjoy a few hours in God's service once a week in this world, it is plain that we could not enjoy an eternity in his service in the world to come.

Expository Thoughts on Luke, 2.90.

Can anyone say that Sunday travelling, except on very rare emergencies, is a work of *mercy*?—Will anyone tell us that Sunday trading, Sunday dinner parties, Sunday excursion-trains on railways, Sunday deliveries of letters and newspapers, are works of *mercy*?—Have servants, and shopmen, and engine-drivers, and coachmen, and clerks, and porters, no souls?

Expository Thoughts on Luke, 2.112.

It is but a few steps from 'no sabbath' to 'no God.'

Expository Thoughts on Luke, 2.363.

Begin with not honouring God's day, and you will soon not honour God's house;—cease to honour God's house, and you will soon cease to honour God's book; cease to honour God's book, and by and by you will give God no honour at all. Let a man lay the foundation of having *no Sabbath*, and I am never surprised if he finishes with the top-stone of *no God.*

Thoughts for Young Men, 66.

Tell the working-classes that if English Sundays are ever turned into days of play and amusement, they will soon become days of labour and work.

Charges and Addresses, 256.

Voltaire was quite right when he said he could never succeed in destroying Christianity unless he destroyed Sunday.

Charges and Addresses, 404-5.

I find him [Jesus] speaking eleven times on the subject of the Sabbath, but it is always to correct the superstitious additions which the Pharisees had made to the law of Moses about observing it, and never to deny the holiness of the day. He no more abolishes the Sabbath, than a man destroys a house when he cleans off the moss or weeds from its roof.

Knots Untied, 337.

One plain rule about the Sabbath is that *it must be kept as a day of rest.* All work of every kind ought to cease as far as possible, both of body and mind. 'Thou shalt not do any work, thou, nor thy son, nor thy daughter, thy man-servant nor thy maid-servant, nor thy cattle, nor thy stranger that is within thy gates.' Works of necessity and mercy may be done. ...

The other great rule about the Sabbath is, that *it must be kept holy.* ... It is not to be a carnal, sensual rest, like that of the worshippers of the golden calf, who 'sat down to eat and drink, and rose up to play' (Exod. 32:6). It is to be emphatically a holy rest. It is to be a rest in which, as far as possible, the affairs of the soul may be attended to, the business of another world minded, and communion with God and Christ kept up. In short, it ought never to be forgotten that it is 'the Sabbath of the LORD our God' (Exod. 20:10).

Knots Untied, 346-47.

SAINTS

How much more easy it is to admire dead saints than living ones.

Expository Thoughts on Luke, 2.39.

SALVATION

We have no warrant for supposing that the aggregate number of those who are lost will prove finally to be greater than the number of the saved. When all the infants who die without knowing good from evil, and all the 'nations of the saved,' who shall be converted after the calling in of the Jews, are added to the ranks of God's elect under the present dispensation, they shall be a multitude that no man can number. They will probably far exceed in number those who are lost.

Expository Thoughts on Luke, 2.101.

The death of Christ was necessary to our salvation. His flesh and blood offered in sacrifice on the cross were 'the life of the world' (John 6:51). Without the death of Christ, so far as we can see, God's law could never have been satisfied,—sin could never have been pardoned,—man could never have been justified before God,—and God could never have shown mercy to man.

Expository Thoughts on Luke, 2.384.

You cannot save that soul of yours, my brother: remember that! You cannot make your own peace with God. You cannot wipe away a single sin. You cannot blot out one of the black records which stand in the book of God against you. You cannot change your own heart. But there is one thing you can do,—you can lose your own soul.

Old Paths, 44.

(a) To be saved, is to be delivered in this present life from the *guilt of sin*, by faith in Jesus Christ, the Saviour. It is to be pardoned, justified, and freed from every charge of sin, by faith in Christ's blood and mediation. Whosoever with his heart believes on the Lord Jesus Christ, is a saved soul. He shall not perish. He shall have eternal life. This is the first part of salvation, and the root of all the rest. But this is not all.

(b) To be saved, is to be delivered in this present life from *the power of sin*, by being born again, and sanctified by Christ's spirit. It is to be freed from the hateful dominion of sin, the world, and the devil, by having a new nature put in us by the Holy Ghost. Whosoever is thus renewed in the spirit of his mind, and converted, is a saved soul. He shall not perish. He shall enter into the glorious kingdom of God. This is the second part of salvation. But this is not all.

(c) To be saved, is to be delivered in the day of judgment, from all *the awful consequences of sin*. It is to be declared blameless, spotless, faultless, and complete in Christ, while others are found guilty, and condemned for ever.

Old Paths, 63-64.

Without believing there is no salvation.

Old Paths, 363.

All who have ever been saved have drawn near to God by this way. From Abel, the first saint that entered Paradise, down to the last infant that died this morning, they have all come to God only by Jesus Christ. 'No man cometh unto the Father but by Christ' (John 14:6).

Old Paths, 411.

Doubtless no one can change his own heart, or wipe away one of his sins, or make himself in the least degree acceptable to God; but I do say that if man could do nothing but sit still, Christ would never have said 'Strive.'

Practical Religion, 28.

You must know the misery and guilt of your own estate by nature. You must experience the power of Christ's atoning blood sprinkled upon your conscience, and making you whole. You must taste the sweetness of peace with God through the mediation of Jesus, and feel the love of a reconciled Father shed abroad in your heart by the Holy Ghost.

Practical Religion, 313.

Think what a mercy it is to have something which the world can neither give nor take away.

Practical Religion, 365.

Be sure that the least drop of the water of life is better than all the rivers of the world.

Practical Religion, 429.

Benefits of Salvation

He whose citizenship is in heaven (Phil. 3:20), who has God for his Father, and Christ for his Elder Brother, angels for his daily guards, and heaven itself for his home, is one that is well provided for.

Practical Religion, 213.

SANCTIFICATION

They are led to prayer. They are led to holiness. This is the beaten path along which the Spirit makes them to travel. Those whom God adopts he always sanctifies.

Practical Religion, 387.

Suffering is a part of the process by which the sons of God are sanctified.

Practical Religion, 391.

The world is not so strong an enemy as you think, if you will only meet it boldly, and use the right weapons.

Upper Room, 122.

SATAN

Let us beware of the devil. We shall always find him at church.

Expository Thoughts on Luke, 1.192.

The wolf does not crave the blood of the lamb more than the devil desires the destruction of souls.

Expository Thoughts on Luke, 2.305.

I remind you that Satan always was a liar. One time he told you it was 'too soon' for religion: and now he tells you it is 'too late.'

Old Paths, 164.

Strategies of the Devil

He will exalt the pleasures of wickedness,—but he will hide from you the sting. He will lift up before your eyes the cross and its painfulness,—but he will keep out of sight the eternal crown. He will promise you everything, as he did to Christ, if you will only serve him (Matt. 4:8). He will even help you to wear a form of religion, if you will only neglect the power (2 Tim. 3:5). He will tell you at the beginning of your lives, it is *too soon* to serve God,—he will tell you at the end, it is *too late.*

Thoughts for Young Men, 13.

The axe in the fable only begged the trees to let him have one little piece of wood to make a handle, and he would never trouble them any more. He got it, and then he soon cut them all down. The devil only wants to get the wedge of a little allowed sin into your heart, and you will soon be all his own.

Thoughts for Young Men, 57.

It is his constant object to wound, hurt, vex, injure, or weaken, if he cannot kill and destroy.

Upper Room, 187.

The great maxim of Satan is, 'Divide and conquer.'

Knots Untied, 265.

SICKNESS

I earnestly entreat all sick believers to remember that they may honour God as much by patient suffering as they can by active work. It often shows more grace to sit still than it does to go to and fro, and perform great exploits.

Practical Religion, 347-48.

Sickness, we must always remember, is no sign that God is displeased with us; nay, more, it is generally sent for the good of our souls. It tends to draw our affections away from this world, and to direct them to things above.

Expository Thoughts on John, 2.167
(also *Power and Sympathy of Christ,* 2).

How much in the history of our lives hinges on little events, and specially on illnesses! Sickness is a sacred thing, and one of God's great ordinances.

Expository Thoughts on John, 2.171
(also *Power and Sympathy of Christ,* 11).

SIN

We take to sin naturally from the very first.

Old Paths, 169.

The best and highest saint is a poor weak creature, even at his best times. Whether he knows it or not, he carries within him an almost boundless capacity of wickedness, however fair and decent his outward conduct may seem. There is no enormity of sin into which he may not run, if he does not watch and pray, and if the grace of God does not hold him up.

Expository Thoughts on Luke, 2.325-26.

Either your sins are UPON YOURSELF, unpardoned, unforgiven, uncleansed, unwashed away,—sinking you daily nearer to hell! Or else your sins are UPON CHRIST, taken away, forgiven, pardoned, blotted out and cleansed away by Christ's precious blood! I am utterly unable to see any third place in which a man's sins can possibly be. I am utterly unable to discover any third alternative. Forgiven or unforgiven,—pardoned or not pardoned,—cleansed away or not cleansed,—this, according to the Bible, is the exact position of everyone's sins. How is it with you? '*Where are your sins?*'.

Old Paths, 163.

Today's sorrow will not wipe off the score of yesterday's sins.

Old Paths, 175.

Forgiven souls *hate* sin. ... It is the serpent which bit them: how should they not shrink from it with horror?

Old Paths, 188.

The abominable thing which God hates.

Practical Religion, 52-53.

There are pleasures in sin no doubt, but they are not real and satisfactory. There is an excitement and short lived enjoyment in the world's ways, beyond all question, but it is joy that leaves a bitter taste behind it.

Practical Religion, 375-76.

Sin is the cause of all the burdens which now press down mankind. Most men know it not, and weary themselves in vain to explain the state of things around them. But sin is the great root and foundation of all sorrow, whatever proud man may think.

Christmas Thoughts, 7.

Every fresh act of sin lessens fear and remorse, hardens our hearts, blunts the edge of our conscience, and increases our evil inclination.

Thoughts for Young Men, 11.

A small leak will sink a great ship, and a small spark will kindle a great fire, and a little allowed sin in like manner will ruin an immortal soul. Take my advice and never spare a little sin. Israel was commanded to slay every Canaanite, both great and small. Act on the same principle, and show no mercy to little sins.

Thoughts for Young Men, 55.

There is nothing finer than the point of a needle, but when it has made a hole, it draws all the thread after it. Remember the apostle's words, 'A little leaven leaveneth the whole lump' (1 Cor. 5:6).

Thoughts for Young Men, 56.

The scars left by youthful sins, even after forgiveness and complete reconciliation with God, are never wholly effaced, and the recollection of them often causes bitter sorrow.

Christian Leaders of the Eighteenth Century, 201.

Sin, in short, is that vast moral disease which affects the whole human race, of every rank and class and name and nation and people and tongue, the plague of rulers and statesmen, the divider of Churches, the destroyer of family happiness, the cause of all the miseries in the world.

Charges and Addresses, 243.

Without confession there is *no salvation.*

Knots Untied, 292.

If a man has learned to feel and acknowledge his sinfulness, he has great reason to thank God. It is a real symptom of health in the inward man.

Knots Untied, 295.

Indwelling Sin

Whether we like to acknowledge it or not, there are within us, at our very best, latent dislike of trouble, secret desire to please man and keep in with the world, carelessness about our private Bible-reading and our prayers, envy and jealousy of others, laziness about doing good, selfishness and desire to have our own way, forgetfulness of the wishes of others, and want of watchfulness over our own besetting sins. All these things are often lying hid within us, and below the surface of our hearts.

Upper Room, 185.

Original Sin

I find men's hearts are everywhere the same, and everywhere wicked. Sin is the family disease of all the children of Adam.

Old Paths, 171.

We hold that a mighty spiritual disease like this requires a mighty spiritual medicine for its cure. We dread giving the slightest countenance to any religious system of dealing with man's soul, which even *seems* to encourage the notion that his deadly wound can be easily healed.

Knots Untied, 5.

All children of Adam born into the world, whatever be their name or nation, are corrupt, wicked, and defiled in the sight of God. Their thoughts, words, ways, and actions are all, more or less, defective and imperfect. Is there no country on the face of the globe where sin does not reign?

Knots Untied, 33.

Sinful Habits

At first they are all like cobwebs. At last they are iron chains.

Old Paths, 394.

Unpardonable Sin

The man whose sins will not be forgiven, is precisely the man who will never seek to have them forgiven. This is exactly the root of his awful disease. He might be pardoned, but he will not seek to be pardoned. He is gospel-hardened and 'twice dead.' His conscience is 'seared with a hot iron' (1 Tim. 4:2).

Expository Thoughts on Luke, 2.50.

The great question of the unpardonable sin, and the possibility of falling into it in modern days, is a distinct branch of the subject, and is not the chief point in the passage before us. That there is such a sin is clear. That it consists of the union of the clearest head-knowledge of the gospel with deliberate rejection of it, and deliberate choice of sin and the world, seems highly probable. That those who are troubled with fear that they have committed it, are just the persons who have not committed it, is the judgment of all the soundest divines. Utter hardness, callousness, and insensibility of conscience, are probably leading characteristics of the man who has sinned the unpardonable sin. He is 'let alone,' and given over to a reprobate mind.

Expository Thoughts on Luke, 2.52.

SLANDER

The accuser of the brethren knows well that character is one of the points in which he can most easily wound a Christian. He knows well that slanders are easily called into existence, greedily received and propagated, and seldom entirely silenced.

Expository Thoughts on Luke, 1.170.

'Slander,' says a Chinese proverb, 'is an insect which has long wings but not feet. It cannot stand, but it can fly.'

Charges and Addresses, 362.

SONG

Let us mark ... *who they were that first praised God, when Christ was born*. They were angels, and not men,—angels who had never sinned, and needed no Saviour,—angels who had not fallen, and required no redeemer, and no atoning blood. The first hymn to the honour of 'God manifest in the flesh,' was sung by 'a multitude of the heavenly host.'

Expository Thoughts on Luke, 1.44.

SOUL

All is not over when the last breath is drawn, and the doctor's last visit has been paid,—when the coffin is screwed down, and the funeral preparations are made,—when 'ashes to ashes and dust to dust' has been pronounced over the grave,—when our place in the world is filled up, and the gap made by our absence from society is no longer noticed. No: all is not over then! The spirit of man still lives on. Everyone has within him an undying soul.

Old Paths, 40.

You may *murder* your soul by running into open sin, and serving lusts and pleasures. Adultery and fornication, drunkenness and revelling, blasphemy and Sabbath-breaking, dishonesty and lying, are all so many short-cuts to perdition.

Old Paths, 44-45.

What should we think of a man who in time of famine fed his dog and starved his child? Should we not say that he was a heartless and unnatural father? Well: take heed that you do not do something like this yourself. Do not forget your soul in your anxiety for your body. Do not, in your concern about the life that now is, forget that which is to come. Do not neglect your soul!

Old Paths, 56.

SOVEREIGNTY OF GOD

He is a God of infinite *power*. He made all things at the beginning. He orders all things according to his will. He casts down the kings of this world in a moment. None can stand against him when he is angry.—Above all, he is a God in whose hands are our lives and all our concerns. He first gave us being. He has kept us alive since we were born. He will remove us when he sees fit, and reckon with us according to our ways. Such is the God with whom we have to do.

Old Paths, 147.

Sovereignty and Human Responsibility

Our salvation is wholly of God. Let that never be forgotten. None but the elect shall be finally saved. 'No man can come unto Christ except the Father draw him' (John 6:44). But our ruin, if we are lost, will be wholly of ourselves. We shall reap the fruit of our own choice. We shall find that we have lost our own souls. Linked between these two principles lies truth which we must maintain firmly, and never let go. There is doubtless deep mystery about it. Our minds are too feeble to understand it now. But we shall understand it all hereafter. God's sovereignty and man's responsibility shall appear perfectly harmonious one day. In the meantime, whatever we doubt, let us never doubt Christ's infinite willingness to save.

Expository Thoughts on Luke, 2.106.

If you are lost, it is not because you could not be saved. If you are lost, it is not because there was no pardon for sinners, no mediator, no high priest, no fountain open for sin and for uncleanness, no open door. It is because you would have your own way, because you would cleave to your sins, because you would not come to Christ, that in Christ you might have life.

Old Paths, 55.

SUFFERING

A suffering Saviour generally has suffering disciples. The Bridegroom was a man of sorrows. The Bride most not be a woman of pleasures and unacquainted with grief. Blessed are they that mourn! Let us not murmur at the cross. This also is a sign of sonship.

Practical Religion, 391.

TEACHING

It may be doubted whether the modern way of teaching Christianity, as a general rule, is sufficiently simple. It is a certain fact that deep reasoning and elaborate arguments are not the weapons by which God is generally pleased to convert souls. Simple plain statements, boldly and solemnly made, and made in such a manner that they are evidently felt and believed by him who makes them, seem to have the most effect on hearts and consciences.

Expository Thoughts on Luke, 1.269.

A minister may speak the truth as it is in Jesus, clearly, forcibly, unanswerably; but if he does not speak it in love, few souls will be won.

Upper Room, 247.

TEMPLE

The mercy seat, the candlestick, the altar of incense, the laver of water, the altar of burnt offering, were all given by God himself to be lively types of good things to come, and to teach us by figures and pictures the glorious gospel of Christ.

Charges and Addresses, 197.

TEMPTATIONS

Unbelief, worldliness, and presumption are three grand engines which he is ever working against the soul of man, and by which he is ever enticing him to do what God forbids, and to run into sin. Let us remember this, and be on our guard. The acts that Satan suggests to us to do, are often in appearance trifling and unimportant. But the principle involved in each of these little acts, we may be sure, is nothing short of rebellion against God. Let us not be ignorant of Satan's devices.

Expository Thoughts on Luke, 1.85-86.

The things of this life form one of the greatest dangers which beset a Christian's path. The money, the pleasures, the daily business of the world, are so many traps to catch souls. Thousands of things, which in themselves are innocent, become, when followed to excess, little better than soul-poisons, and helps to hell. Open sin is not the only thing that ruins souls.

Expository Thoughts on Luke, 1.193.

THEOLOGY

In matters of theology, 'the old is better.'

Light from Old Times, 351.

Charity in Theology

On the other hand, at the same time, I desire to raise a warning voice against the growing tendency to be dogmatical about things which are not necessary to salvation, to be positive where the Bible is silent, to condemn and anathematize those whom God has not condemned, and to exalt things in different and secondary to a level with the primary verities and weightier matters of the gospel. … Let us always remember it is possible to be too narrow as well as too broad.

Charges and Addresses, 68.

Controversy in Theology

It is a pity, no doubt, that there should be so much controversy; but it is also a pity that human nature should be so bad as it is, and that the devil should be loose in the world. It was a pity that Arius taught error about Christ's person: but it would have been a greater pity if Athanasius had not opposed him. It was a pity Tetzel went about preaching up the Pope's indulgences: it would have been a far greater pity if Luther had not withstood him. Controversy, in fact, is one of the conditions under which truth in every age has to be defended and maintained, and it is nonsense to ignore it.

Light from Old Times, 391-92.

False Doctrine

There is an intolerance which is downright praiseworthy,—that is, the intolerance of false teaching in the pulpit. Who would ever think of tolerating a little poison given to him day by day?

Knots Untied, 63.

False doctrine does not meet men face to face, and proclaim that it is false. It does not blow a trumpet before it, and endeavour openly to turn us away from the truth as it is in Jesus. It does not come before men in broad day, and summon them to surrender. It approaches us secretly, quietly, insidiously, plausibly, and in such a way as to disarm man's suspicion, and throw him off his guard. It is the wolf in sheep's clothing, and Satan in the garb of an angel of light, who have always proved the most dangerous foes of the church of Christ.

Knots Untied, 374.

Every heresy began at one time with some little departure from the truth. There is only a little seed of error needed to create a great tree.

Knots Untied, 377.

Beware of supposing that a teacher of religion is to be trusted, because, although he holds some unsound views, he yet 'teaches a great deal of truth.' Such a teacher is precisely the man to do you harm: poison is always most dangerous when it is given in small doses and mixed with wholesome food.

Knots Untied, 384.

THIRTY-NINE ARTICLES

Let us set our foot down firmly on the wise and moderate principles laid down in our Articles, and refuse to go one inch beyond.

Charges and Addresses, 254.

Reason itself points out that the Prayer-book and Articles were meant to teach the same doctrines, and that no interpretation which makes them jar and contradict one another can be correct. Lord Chatham's famous dictum, that the Church of England has a popish Liturgy, and Arminian clergy, and a Calvinistic set of Articles, was doubtless very smart, but it was not true.

Knots Untied, 78.

Evangelical clergymen yield to none in willingness to give rightful honour to baptism and the Lord Supper. All we say is, that grace is not tied to the sacraments, and that a man may receive them, and be done the better for it. And what is all this but the doctrine of the Thirty-nine Articles?

Knots Untied, 89-90.

As for clergymen, if I had my own way I would require them to read the Articles publicly in church once every year.

Knots Untied, 94.

TIME

Think of the *shortness of time*. You will soon be gone. You will have no opportunity for works of mercy in another world. In heaven there will be no ignorant people to instruct, and no unconverted to reclaim. Whatever you do must be done now. Oh, when are you going to begin? Awake! be zealous, and repent.

Practical Religion, 196

TITHING/GIVING

Let us remember, that although Christ's work does not depend on our money, yet Christ is pleased to test the reality of our grace by allowing us to help him. If we cannot find it in our hearts to give anything to Christ's cause, we may well doubt the reality of our faith and charity.

Expository Thoughts on Luke, 2.263.

Whoever found himself really poorer by lending to the Lord?

Expository Thoughts on Luke, 2.263.

TOLERANCE

'Forbearance and toleration' are fine, high-sounding words; but if they mean that every clergyman is to be allowed to do what he likes, they seem to me the certain forerunner of confusion, division, and disruption.

Charges and Addresses, 30.

TOTAL DEPRAVITY

What are we all but lepers spiritually in the sight of God? Sin is the deadly sickness by which we are all affected. It has eaten into our constitution. It has infected all our faculties. Heart, conscience, mind, and will, all are diseased by sin. From the sole of our foot to the crown of our head, there is no soundness about us, but wounds, and bruises, and putrefying sores (Isa. 1:6). Such is the state in which we are born. Such is the state in which we naturally live. We are in one sense dead long before we are laid in the grave. Our bodies may be healthy and active, but our souls are by nature dead in trespasses and sins.

Expository Thoughts on Luke, 1.105.

In vain the bread and water of life are offered to him: his soul is neither hungry for the one, nor thirsty for the other. In vain he is advised to flee to the great Physician: his soul is unconscious of its disease;—why should he go? In vain you put a price into his hand to buy wisdom: the mind of his soul wanders,—he is like the lunatic, who calls straws a crown, and dust diamonds; he says, 'I am rich, and increased with goods, and have need of nothing.' Alas, there is nothing so sad as the utter corruption of our nature! There is nothing so painful as the anatomy of a dead soul.

Knots Untied, 134.

TRIALS

Let us say to ourselves in the darkest hour of trial, 'This also is ordered by him who gave Christ to die for my sins. It cannot be wrong. It is done in love. It must be well'.

Old Paths, 362.

We may be no less sure that poverty and trial are no certain proof of God's anger. They are often blessings in disguise. They are always sent in love and wisdom. They often serve to wean man from the world. They teach him to set his affections on things above.

Practical Religion, 301-2.

The world, nearly all men agree, is full of trouble. It is a true saying that we come into life crying, and pass through it complaining, and leave it disappointed.

Upper Room, 48.

By them he keeps us humble. By them he draws us to himself. By them he sends us to our Bibles. By them he teaches us to pray. By them he shows us our need of Christ. By them he weans us from the world. By them he prepares us for 'a city which hath foundations,' in which there will be no disappointments, no tears, and no sin. It is no special mark of God's favour when Christians have no trials.

Upper Room, 220-21.

TRUTH

Let us take comfort in the thought that in the long run of years the truth will always prevail. Its advocates may often be feeble, and their arguments very weak. But there is an inherent strength in the cause itself which keeps it alive. Bold infidels like Porphyry, and Julian, and Hobbes, and Hume, and Voltaire, and Payne arise from time to time and make a stir in the world. But they produce no lasting impression. They pass away like the Sadducees and go to their own place. The great evidences of Christianity remain like the Pyramids, unshaken and unmoved. The 'gates of hell' shall never prevail against Christ's truth (Matt. 16:18).

Expository Thoughts on Luke, 2.252.

There is a time coming when many will repent too late, and believe too late,—sorrow for sin too late, and begin to pray too late,—be anxious about salvation too late, and long for heaven too late. Myriads shall wake up in another world, and be convinced of truths which on earth they refused to believe. Earth is the only place in God's creation where there is any infidelity. Hell itself is nothing but truth known too late.

Expository Thoughts on Luke, 2.100-1.

Whose words, after all, are true? Whose estimate is correct? Whose judgment will stand at the last day? By whose standard will all be tried, before they receive their eternal sentence? Before whose bar will the current opinions of the world be tested and weighed at last? These are the only questions which ought to influence our conduct; and to these questions the Bible returns a plain answer. The counsel of the Lord,—it alone shall stand forever. The word of Christ,—it alone shall judge man at the last day.

Expository Thoughts on Luke, 2.155.

An ounce of facts is better than a pound of theories.

Charges and Addresses, 322.

UNBELIEF

Few sins appear to be so peculiarly provoking to God as the sin of unbelief. None certainly have called down such heavy judgments on men. It is a practical denial of God's almighty power to doubt whether he can do a thing, when he undertakes to do it.—It is giving the lie to God to doubt whether he means to do a thing, when he has plainly promised that it shall be done.

Expository Thoughts on Luke, 1.15.

The plain truth is, that the natural heart of man hates God. The carnal mind is enmity against God. It dislikes his law, his gospel, and his people. It will always find some excuse for not believing and obeying. The doctrine of repentance is too strict for it! The doctrine of faith and grace is too easy for it! John the Baptist goes too much out of the world! Jesus Christ goes too much into the world! And so the heart of man excuses itself for sitting still in its sins.

Expository Thoughts on Luke, 1.176.

Those who reject the gospel, and remain impenitent and unbelieving, are not merely objects of pity and compassion, but deeply guilty and blameworthy in God's sight. God called, but they refused. God spoke to them, but they would not regard. The condemnation of the unbelieving will be strictly just. Their blood will be upon their own heads. The Judge of all the earth will do right.

Expository Thoughts on Luke, 1.270.

We do not sufficiently realize the corruption of human nature. We do not see the full virulence of the disease by which all Adam's children are infected, and the small number of those who are saved.—Have we faith, however weak and small? Let us praise God for the privilege. Who are we that God should have made us to differ? Let us watch against unbelief. The root of it often lies within us even after the tree is cut down.

Expository Thoughts on Luke, 2.25.

Unconverted people are never really happy. Under a profession of high spirits and cheerfulness, they are often ill at ease within. Thousands of them are sick at heart, dissatisfied with themselves, weary of their own ways, and thoroughly uncomfortable.

Expository Thoughts on Luke, 2.136.

Without the Spirit he is without Christ. Without Christ he is without God. Without God the Father, God the Son, and God the Spirit, he is in imminent danger.

Old Paths, 268.

Would heaven's everlasting praise suit the taste of those who can hardly spare a few minutes in a week for private religion, even for prayer?

Old Paths, 309.

The old marble statues in many a cathedral church have heard the substance of thousands of sermons. Yet they never show any feeling. Not a muscle of their marble faces ever shrinks or moves. It is just the same with the natural heart. It is utterly destitute of spiritual feeling.

Old Paths, 325.

Without God they rise in the morning, and without God they lie down at night. They ask for nothing; they confess nothing; they return thanks for nothing; they seek nothing. They are all dying creatures, and yet they are not even on speaking terms with their Maker and their Judge!

Practical Religion, 31.

None are so blind as those who will not see.

Expository Thoughts on John, 2.170
(also *Power and Sympathy of Christ,* 8).

UNCONVERTED

He that boasts of liberty, while he is enslaved by lusts and passions, is going down to hell with a lie in his right hand.

Practical Religion, 212.

You are in the midst of a failing, sorrowful world, and you have no real source of comfort, or refuge for a time of need. You are a dying creature, and you are not ready to die. You have sins, and they are not forgiven. You are going to be judged, and you are not prepared to meet God: you might be, but you refuse to use the one only Mediator and Advocate. You love the world better than Christ. You refuse the great Friend of sinners, and you have no friend in heaven to plead your cause. Yes: it is sadly true! You are a poor, miserable being. It matters nothing what your income is: without Christ's friendship you are very poor.

Practical Religion, 329.

Yes! you may have rare intellectual gifts and high mental attainments: you may sway kingdoms by your counsel, move millions by your pen, or keep crowds in breathless attention by your tongue; but if you have never submitted yourself to the yoke of Christ, and never honoured his gospel by heartfelt reception of it, you are nothing in his sight.

Practical Religion, 414.

I have learned, by the painful experience of the third of a century, that people may go on for years attending God's house, and yet never feel their sins, or desire to be saved. The cares of this world, the love of pleasure, the 'lust of other things,' choke the good seed every Sunday, and make it unfruitful. They come to church with hearts as cold as the stone pavement on which they walk.

Upper Room, 107-8.

UNFORGIVENESS

A spiteful quarrelsome Christian is a scandal to his profession. It is very hard to believe that such an one has ever sat at the foot of the cross, and has ever considered how he is praying against himself every time he uses the Lord's Prayer. Is he not saying as it were, 'Father, do not forgive me my trespasses at all'?

Old Paths, 190.

UNHAPPINESS

A man of wit and pleasure shall be our next witness: I mean Lord Chesterfield. He shall speak for himself: his own words in a letter shall be his testimony: 'I have seen the silly round of business and pleasure, and have done with it all. I have enjoyed all the pleasures of the world, and consequently know their futility, and do not regret their loss.'

Practical Religion, 228.

UNIVERSALISM

What was the use of God's Son becoming incarnate, agonizing in Gethsemane, and dying on the cross to make atonement, if men can be finally saved without believing on him?

Charges and Addresses, 259.

UNITY

About sin and salvation, about repentance, and faith, and holiness, there is a mighty unity among all believers, of every name, and nation, and people, and tongue. Let us make much of these points in our own personal religion. These, after all, are the principal things which we shall think of in the hour of death, and the day of judgment. On other matters we must agree to differ. It will signify little at the last day what we thought about fasting, and eating, and drinking, and ceremonies. Did we repent, and bring forth fruits meet for repentance? Did we behold the Lamb of God by faith, and receive him as our Saviour? All, of every church, who are found right on these points, will be saved. All, of every church, who are found wrong on these points, will be lost for evermore.

Expository Thoughts on Luke, 1.119.

WARNINGS

The father who sees his son tottering toward the brink of a precipice, and as he sees him cries out sharply, 'Stop, stop!'—does not that father love his son?—The tender mother who sees her infant on the point of eating some poisonous berry, and cries out sharply, 'Stop, stop! Put it down!'—does not that mother love that child?—It is indifference which lets people alone, and allows them to go on every one in his own way. It is love, tender love, which warns, and raises the cry of alarm. … The words, 'Except ye repent, ye shall all perish,' may seem at first sight stern and severe. But they are words of love, and may be the means of delivering precious souls from hell.

Old Paths, 379-80.

The time is short. The end of all things is at hand. The shadows are lengthening. The sun is going down. The night cometh when no man can work. The great white throne will soon be set. The judgment will begin. The books will be opened. Awake, and come out from the world while it is called today.

Practical Religion, 288.

WEALTH

Kings must one day leave their palaces. Rich men must one day leave their money and lands. They only hold them till they die.—But the poorest saint on earth has a treasure of which he will never be deprived. The grace of God, and the favour of Christ, are riches which no man can take from him. They will go with him to the grave when he dies. They will rise with him in the resurrection morning, and be his to all eternity.

Expository Thoughts on Luke, 1.295.

It is plain matter of fact, that comparatively few rich men are to be found in the way of life. For one thing, riches incline their possessors to pride, self-will, self-indulgence, and love of the world. For another thing, the rich man is seldom dealt with faithfully about his soul. He is generally flattered and fawned upon. 'The rich hath many friends' (Prov. 14:20). Few persons have the courage to tell him the whole truth. His good points are grossly exaggerated. His bad points are glossed over, palliated, and excused. The result is, that while his heart is choked up with the things of the world, his eyes are blinded to his own real condition. What right have we to wonder that a rich man's salvation is a hard thing?

Expository Thoughts on Luke, 2.203-4.

No one is too bad to be saved, or beyond the power of Christ's grace. We are told of a wealthy publican becoming a disciple of Christ. A more unlikely event we cannot well imagine! We see the 'camel passing through the eye of a needle,' and the 'rich man entering the kingdom of God.' We behold a plain proof that 'all things are possible with God.' We see a covetous tax-gatherer transformed into a liberal Christian!

Expository Thoughts on Luke, 2.216.

It is an utter mistake to suppose that *riches alone* can give happiness. They can enable a man to command and possess everything but inward peace! They cannot buy a cheerful spirit and a light heart.

Practical Religion, 224.

We may be very sure that riches and worldly greatness are no certain marks of God's favour. They are often, on the contrary, a snare and hindrance to a man's soul. They make him love the world and forget God.

Practical Religion, 301.

WEARINESS

He who made atonement for us on the cross is one who 'can be touched with the feeling of our infirmities' (Heb. 4:15). To be weary of working for God is sinful, but to be wearied and worn in doing God's work is no sin at all.

Expository Thoughts on Luke, 1.200.

WESLEY, JOHN

[William] Romaine's death-bed was a beautiful illustration of the truth of John Wesley's saying, 'Our people die well! The world may find fault with our opinions, but the world cannot deny that our people die well.'

Christian Leaders of the Eighteenth Century, 158

John Wesley's memorial tablet in Westminster Abbey contains a striking saying, 'God buries his workmen, but carries on his work.'

Charges and Addresses, 70.

The blind stupidity with which John Wesley was treated was a disaster to our Church. We ought to have taken a leaf out of his book. Never will things go well with the Church of England until every individual member realizes that he has a duty to do to Christ and his Church, and keeps that duty continually in view.

Charges and Addresses, 277.

WHITEFIELD, GEORGE

When the occupants of the episcopal bench were troubled by the rapid spread of Whitefield's influence, it was gravely suggested in high quarters that the best way to stop his influence was to make him a bishop.

Christian Leaders of the Eighteenth Century, 7.

The doctrines of free grace, once thoroughly grasped, took deep root in his heart, and became, as it were, bone of his bone and flesh of his flesh. Of all the little band of Oxford Methodists, none seem to have got hold so soon of clear views of Christ's gospel as he did, and none kept it so unwaveringly to the end.

Christian Leaders of the Eighteenth Century, 23.

He loved the Church in which he had been ordained; he gloried in her Articles; he used her Prayer-book with pleasure. But the Church did not love him, and so lost the use of his services. The plain truth is, that the Church of England of that day was not ready for a man like Whitefield. The Church was too much asleep to understand him, and was vexed at a man who would not keep still and let the devil alone.

Christian Leaders of the Eighteenth Century, 28.

He did not get up to talk about his party, his cause, his interest or his office. He was perpetually telling you about your sins, your heart, Jesus Christ, the Holy Ghost, the absolute need of repentance, faith, and holiness, in the way that the Bible presents these mighty subjects. 'Oh, the righteousness of Jesus Christ!' he would often say; 'I must be excused if I mention it in almost all my sermons.' Preaching of this kind is the preaching that God delights to honour.

Christian Leaders of the Eighteenth Century, 39.

Even the Erskines, in Scotland, wanted him to preach for no other denomination but their own—viz., the Secession Church. He asked them, 'Why only for them?' and received the notable answer that 'they were the Lord's people.' This was more than Whitefield could stand. He asked 'if there were no other Lord's people but themselves'; he told them, 'if all others were the devil's people, they certainly had more need to be preached to'; and he wound up by informing them, that 'if the Pope himself would lend him his pulpit, he would gladly proclaim the righteousness of Christ in it'.

Christian Leaders of the Eighteenth Century, 47.

WISDOM

We must seek to have knowledge as well as zeal. Zeal without knowledge is an army without a general, and a ship without a rudder. We must pray that we may understand how to make a right application of Scripture. The word is no doubt 'a light to our feet, and a lantern to our path.' But it must be the word rightly handled, and properly applied.

Expository Thoughts on Luke, 1.255.

In all doubtful cases we should first pray for wisdom and sound judgment. If prayer is worth anything, it must be specially valuable when we desire to do right, but do not see our way.

Practical Religion, 284.

WORLD

When I speak of 'the world' … I mean those people who think only, or chiefly, of this world's things, and neglect the world to come,—the people who are always thinking more of earth than of heaven, more of time than of eternity, more of the body than of the soul, more of pleasing man than of pleasing God.

Practical Religion, 269.

Are you overcoming the world, or are you overcome by it? Do you know what it is to come out from the world and be separate, or are you yet entangled by it, and conformed to it?

Practical Religion, 288.

The fetters of the world are often invisible. We are dragged downward insensibly, and are like one who sleeps in a boat, and knows not that he is drifting, gently drifting, towards the falls.

Upper Room, 126.

Happy, indeed, is that Christian who can be in the world and yet not of the world,—who can do his duty in it, and yet not be conformed to it,—who can pass through it unmoved by its smiles or its frowns, its flattery or its enmity.

Upper Room, 186.

The world is never won by trimming, and compromising, by facing both ways, and trying to please all.

Knots Untied, 23.

WORSHIP

Tell me what a man does in the matter of Bible reading and praying, in the matter of Sunday, public worship, and the Lord's supper, and I will soon tell you what he is, and on which road he is travelling.

Practical Religion, 13.

Popularity obtained by pandering to the senses or the sentiment of our hearers is not worth anything. Worshippers who are not content with the Bible, the cross of Christ, simple prayers and simple praise, are worshippers of little value. It is useless to try to please them, because their spiritual taste is diseased.

Knots Untied, 24.

I believe the last day will show that wherever God has had a people he has always had a congregation. His servants, however few in number, have always assembled themselves together, and approached their heavenly Father in company. They have been taught to do it for many wise reasons, partly to bear a public testimony to the world, partly to strengthen, cheer, help, encourage, and comfort one another, and above all, to train and prepare them for the general assembly in heaven.

Worship: Its Priority, Principles, and Practices, 5-6.

True spiritual worship will affect a man's *heart and conscience*. It will make him feel more keenly the sinfulness of sin, and his own particular personal corruption. It will deepen his humility.

Worship: Its Priority, Principles, and Practices, 26.

True spiritual worship will continually increase the *holiness* of a man's life. It will make him every year more watchful over tongue, and temper, and time, and behaviour in every relation of life. The true worshipper's conscience becomes annually more tender. The false worshipper's becomes annually more seared and more hard.

Worship: Its Priority, Principles, and Practices, 27.

The day is coming when there shall be a congregation that shall never break up, and a Sabbath that shall never end, a song of praise that shall never cease, and an assembly that shall never be dispersed. In that assembly shall be found all who have 'worshipped God in spirit' upon earth.

Worship: Its Priority, Principles, and Practices, 28.

Liturgical Forms of Worship

The misuse of a thing is no argument against the right use of it.

Practical Religion, 256.

Ritualism in Worship

We hold that human nature is so easily led astray, and so thoroughly inclined to idolatry, that ornament in Christian worship should be used with a very sparing hand. We firmly believe that the tendency of excessive ornament, and a theatrical ceremonial, is to defeat the primary end for which worship was established, to draw away men's minds from Christ, and to make them walk by sight and not by faith.

Knots Untied, 14.

YOUTH

By the shoot, we judge of the tree,—by the blossoms we judge of the fruit,—by the spring we judge of the harvest,—by the morning we judge of the day,—and by the character of the young man, we may generally judge what he will be when he grows up.

Young men, be not deceived. Think not you can, at will, serve lusts and pleasures in your beginning, and then go and serve God with ease at your latter end. Think not you can live with Esau, and then die with Jacob.

Thoughts for Young Men, 9.

What youth sows, old age must reap.

Thoughts for Young Men, 16-17.

Do not be too confident in your own judgment. Cease to be sure that you are always right, and others wrong. Be distrustful of your own opinion, when you find it contrary to that of older men than yourselves, and specially to that of your own parents.

Thoughts for Young Men, 22.

ZEAL

Zeal in religion is a burning desire to please God, to do his will, and to advance his glory in the world in every possible way.

Practical Religion, 174.

Furthermore, if zeal be true, *it will be joined to a deep humility*. A truly zealous man will be last to discover the greatness of his own attainments.

Practical Religion, 184.

Zeal does not stand poring over difficulties, but simply says, 'Here are souls perishing, and something *shall* be done.'

Practical Religion, 190.

It was a solemn saying of old Bernard when he said that 'Satan would rise up in judgment against some people at the last day, because he had shown more zeal to ruin souls than they had to save them.'

Practical Religion, 196.

Bibliography

All titles listed are published by the Banner of Truth Trust.

Charges and Addresses (2024)
Christmas Thoughts (2023)
Christian Leaders of the Eighteenth Century (2020)
Expository Thoughts on the Gospels, 7 vols. (2023)
Holiness (2023)
Is All Scripture Inspired? (2017)
Knots Untied (2023)
Light from Old Times (2024)
Old Paths (2024)
Practical Religion (2024)
Simplicity in Preaching (2020)
The Power and Sympathy of Christ (2018)
Thoughts For Young Men (2024)
Upper Room (2022)
Worship: Its Priority, Principles, and Practices (2021)

BANNER *of* TRUTH

The Banner of Truth Trust originated in 1957 in London. The founders believed that much of the best literature of historic Christianity had been allowed to fall into oblivion and that, under God, its recovery could well lead not only to a strengthening of the church, but to true revival.

Interdenominational in vision, this publishing work is now international, and our lists include a number of contemporary authors, together with classics from the past. The translation of these books into many languages is encouraged.

A monthly magazine, *The Banner of Truth*, is also published, and further information about this, and all our other publications, may be found on our website, banneroftruth.org, or by contacting the offices below:

Head Office:
3 Murrayfield Road
Edinburgh
EH12 6EL
United Kingdom

Email: info@banneroftruth.co.uk

North America Office:
610 Alexander Spring Road
Carlisle, PA 17015
United States of America

Email: info@banneroftruth.org